WINGS OF DESIRE

CHRISTIAN ROGOWSKI

T0385644

CAMDEN HOUSE

First published 2019 by Camden House

Camden House is an imprint of Boydell & Brewer Inc.
668 Mt. Hope Avenue, Rochester, NY 14620, USA
www.camden-house.com
and of Boydell & Brewer Limited
PO Box 9, Woodbridge, SuffolkI P12 3DF, UK
www.boydellandbrewer.com

ISBN-13: 978-1-64014-037-0
ISBN-10: 1-64014-037-9

All images from *Wings of Desire* directed by Wim Wenders
© 2017 WIM WENDERS STIFTUNG—ARGOS FILMS

Library of Congress Cataloging-in-Publication Data

Names: Rogowski, Christian, 1956– author.
Title: Wings of desire / Christian Rogowski.
Description: Rochester, New York : Camden House, [2019]
    | Series: Camden House German filmc lassics | Includes
bibliographical references.
Identifiers: LCCN 2019020291| ISBN 9781640140370 (pbk.)
    | ISBN 1640140379 (pbk.)
Subjects: LCSH: Himmel über Berlin (Motion picture)
Classification: LCC PN1997.2.H565 R64 2019 | DDC
    791.43/72—dc23 LC record available at https://lccn.loc.
    gov/2019020291

Wings of Desire

Why does my heart ache when it misses a beat?
—Propaganda, "Dr. Mabuse," 1984

Introduction: Angels and Demons

Wings of Desire, written and directed by Wim Wenders with the help of Austrian author Peter Handke, has many passionate admirers, as well as a few equally passionate detractors. The story of two angels in 1980s West Berlin, one of whom, Damiel, decides to forfeit eternal life for love of a woman, the beautiful trapeze artist Marion, resonates with diverse audiences across the world to the point of it having become a kind of cult film. Upon its world premiere, on May 10, 1987 at the Cannes Film Festival, Wenders received an award as best director. The film is widely regarded as a masterpiece of German cinema—the "Taste of Cinema" website ranks it seventh on its list of the thirty most important German films. Its impact, domestically and internationally, is gauged among other things by the fact that it spawned an—ill-fated—US-American remake, *The City of Angels* (directed by Brad Silberling, 1998) starring Meg Ryan and Nicolas Cage, which transposes the main story into contemporary Los Angeles. It also triggered a perhaps equally ill-fated sequel, directed by Wenders himself, without Handke's involvement, *Faraway, So Close!* (*In weiter Ferne, so nah!*, 1993), that traces the story of the other angel, Cassiel. In the fall of 1992, *Wings of Desire* was the first feature film to be broadcast on the new Franco-German cultural TV

Angel Damiel about to turn human: his footprints in the "Death Strip."

channel, *arte*. Irish rock legend Van Morrison set the film's signature poem, "When the Child was a Child," to music, released as "Song of Being a Child" on his compilation album, *The Philosopher's Stone* (1998). A documentary about young people living in the drab concrete tenements of a formerly East German Berlin suburb pays ironic homage to the German original title of Wenders's film, *Der Himmel über Berlin* (the sky / heaven over Berlin), with its laconic title, *Der Himmel über Marzahn* (directed by Habib Jawadi, 2008). More recently, on the occasion of Wenders's seventieth birthday in 2015, his film was turned into a graphic novel by Sebastian and Lorenzo Tome. In Peter Chelsom's science-fiction drama, *The Space Between* (2017), it is after watching *Wings of Desire* on video that young Gardner Elliot (Asa Butterfield), born and raised on Mars, decides, inspired by Damiel's transformation, that he wants to escape the "East Texas" space station to live on earth.

In February 2018, a painstakingly restored version of *Wings of Desire* in ultra-high digital resolution premiered at the Berlin Film Festival to great acclaim. In his presentation there, Wim Wenders noted that the 4K restoration is superior in visual quality to the original version released in 1987. Reporting for the American magazine *Variety*, Andrew Horn summarized Wenders's description of the challenges confronted in the digital frame-by-frame restoration:

> "we shot three-quarters of it in black & white and one-quarter in color," Wenders explains. "They were intercut in each and every reel, and that's where the trouble began." In order to marry the two formats, including seamless transitions, the film had to go through several generations of interpositive and internegative, losing quality with every step, to create the final negatives used for release. "As beautiful as it might have looked in Cannes '87," Wenders adds, "every print ever since is six generations removed."[1]

A similar dynamic applies in the re-edit of the multi-channel, layered soundtrack. In April 2018, the film was re-released in digitally restored and enhanced visual and audio quality to German and international cinemas, attesting to the enduring fascination exuded by the film. More than three decades after its original release viewers can now enjoy a painstakingly restored replica of the film that is, to quote a famous U2 song, "even better than the real thing."

The film's main poetic conceit, involving two angels who bear witness to people's everyday lives and aspirations in the western half of a divided Berlin, makes for a multidimensional film that addresses a wide variety of complex issues. These include: issues of German identity and the lingering impact of National Socialism as a demonic, palpable presence; the Cold War division of Germany; the reintegration into German cultural life of émigrés returning from exile; the politics of remembrance; film and historical witnessing; questions of childhood dreams and emotional fulfillment; the possibility of understanding and love between men and women; interpersonal relations in an alienated and alienating postmodern urban landscape; and a fraught ambivalence concerning the impact of Anglo-American popular culture on contemporary German society.

Why, one may ask, has *Wings of Desire* attained special status among cineastes and "regular" moviegoers alike, despite having also become the object of considerable controversy? French critic Gérard Lefort hailed the film as "one of the most beautiful films one has ever seen" yet it was famously dismissed in the *New Yorker* as "postmodern kitsch" by American critic Pauline Kael.[2] African American social theorist bell hooks famously found fault with the film's universalism, which, in her estimation, extends to whites only.[3] To be sure, as we will see, the film's effort to wrestle with the racially charged demons of Germany's violent past is fraught with problems. All the same, *Wings of Desire* is a life-affirming film that seeks to envelop its viewers in a spirit of awe, love, and compassion. Many aspects of the film—its apolitical overtones, its often ponderous philosophizing, its gender dynamics, its tendency towards mysticism, and its occasional preachiness—strike problematic notes and many issues remain unresolved. The multilayered, multidimensional collage of images and sounds produces multiple interpretations that cannot quite coalesce into a unified whole. Yet, at the same time, there are few films that have as visceral and immediate an impact on the viewer as *Wings of Desire*, the preponderance of its poetic images and emotionally powerful, potentially heart-stopping moments largely bypassing the brain and aiming directly at the viewer's heart.

Whatever ostensible flaws *Wings of Desire* may have can be viewed as the reverse side of its undeniable strengths: the film seeks to connect with its audience in a spirit of compassion, to create a sense of shared experience, to contribute toward establishing a sense of community—noble, if perhaps foolhardy, sentiments in our increasingly fragmented, restless societies, and aspirations that perhaps cannot always escape the risk of turning into problematic cliché. The film represents a daring effort to answer existential questions in a world suspicious of spiritual answers, an ambitious exercise in the cinematic sublime in an age of increasing image overload, a testament to a sustained effort aimed at overcoming cynicism and indifference. It is a film that celebrates the possibility of self-fashioning and new beginnings. It is a film that seeks to make us abandon our mindless busy-ness, to become attentive to the world around us, to overcome conflict, to reconnect with one another, and rediscover a sense of joy in life. And it is a film that invites and teaches its audience to care, about one another and about the world. What could be wrong with that? Indeed, as Elvis Costello would have it, in the words of Nick Lowe, "What's so funny about peace, love, and understanding?" But first things first.

Pale Shadows: The Half and the Whole

In 1987, both East and West Berlin celebrated the city's 750th anniversary. That is, parallel and competing celebrations were held on both sides of the Wall, with both halves claiming to represent the city as a whole. *Wings of Desire* received its German gala premiere in this context, on October 27, 1987, at West Berlin's prestigious Zoo-Palast cinema. The screening was one of the highlights of the year-long anniversary celebrations.

In a sense, the eastern part had a more legitimate claim to the city's history, since this is where the district of Mitte, the historical center of the city, is located. Yet in many ways, even before the Cold War and before the Wall was constructed in 1961, the city had always been divided in two: its origins go back to the twelfth century when two small communities merged, a market town called Berlin that covered the area now called the Museum Island and the Nikolaiviertel, and a farming village called Cölln, located on the left bank of the river Spree. Likewise, with the expansion of the city during the second half of the nineteenth century, two distinct centers emerged, the traditional downtown surrounding Alexanderplatz in the east, and the new commercial center in the west, around the Kaiser-Wilhelm-Memorial Church. In 1920, when various suburbs and adjacent municipalities were incorporated into the city to create Greater Berlin, a sprawling metropolis of some four million people, the city had two formerly royal residences—the Stadtschloß in the east, and the summer palace in the western suburb of Charlottenburg; two main boulevards—the traditionally splendid Unter den Linden in the east and the upscale shopping promenade Kurfürstendamm in the west; two opera houses—the Court (later State) Opera in the east, and the municipal opera house, now the Deutsche Oper, in the Charlottenburg district; and it had two main railway stations—Bahnhof Friedrichstraße in the east and Bahnhof Zoo in the west. From that perspective, the city's division after 1945 by the victorious powers into two halves, with the Soviet occupation zone comprising the eastern part and the American, British, and French zones jointly comprising the western one, could draw upon already existing historical, social, and cultural demarcations. Moreover, the postwar division necessitated the duplication of further institutions and resources that reinforced existing divisions, such as the founding of the Free University in the West, to complement Humboldt University in the East, or the construction of two airports, West Berlin's Tegel and East Berlin's Schönefeld, when Tempelhof airport, which ended up in the American zone, became too small for the West and inaccessible to the East. Most significantly, perhaps, for Wenders's film, the Staatsbibliothek (State Library) near Potsdamer Platz, which in the film serves as the angels' main residence, was built in the 1970s as the western complement to the venerable old Staatsbibliothek located on East Berlin's Unter den Linden boulevard.

By and large, before the Second World War the eastern parts of the city center were associated with the imperial past and working-class neighborhoods, and the western parts with middle-class culture and commerce. After the war, the nodal point between the two traditional halves, Potsdamer Platz, once the busiest traffic intersection in continental Europe, became an urban wasteland, a vast empty expanse of fallow land split by the Wall, inaccessible from the East and undesirable to the West. The once bustling center of a vibrant metropolis had deteriorated into a pale shadow of its former self, between two pale shadows of the city's former selves. Buried in the rubble, little remained of the various layers of Berlin's past that made up its former glory, as the heart of Prussia, the capital of the *Kaiserreich*, the cauldron of Weimar German culture, and the power center of Nazi Germany. If, in a sense, the city no longer existed, the question facing the 1987 anniversary celebrations concerned what exactly could and should be celebrated.

Much like the anniversary celebrations as a whole, the auspicious occasion of the premiere of *Wings of Desire* was fraught with political ironies and historical symbolism: the Zoo-Palast movie theater at which the gala premiere was held, a drab brutalist 1950s picture palace, had replaced the famous Ufa-Palast am Zoo, where many of the most significant German films of the Weimar and pre-Second World War period had opened, including Fritz Lang's legendary *Metropolis* (1927) and Leni Riefensthal's notorious *Triumph of the Will* (1935). Like the rest of the divided city, the new movie palace was but a pale shadow of its former, glamorous self. Divided Berlin, in celebrating itself in duplicate, was a kind of simulacrum of itself, a feeble imitation and a painful reminder of what once had been. With its suggestion of unity above a divided surface, the film's German title, *Der Himmel über Berlin*—"the sky / heaven over Berlin"— seems like a direct response to a famous short novel by celebrated East German author Christa Wolf, *Der geteilte Himmel* (*Divided Heaven*, 1963), which was filmed in 1964 by director Konrad Wolf for East Germany's DEFA studios. Set in 1961, when the Wall was built, it features a young couple forced to decide upon their future— Manfred, the young scientist, seeks economic opportunities and upward mobility in the West, while Rita, still a student, stays in the East, ambivalently committed to the socialist project of building a better society. The novel's title, "Divided Heaven," seems to suggest that the crisis in the relationship of the young couple, revolving around psychological and ideological differences, preceded and mirrors the political division of the city that the Wall made manifest in stone. In a key scene, the two obliquely reflect on the division of Germany, with Manfred noting, "The sky, at least, they can't divide," to which Rita softly responds, "No, it is the sky that divides first."[4] Unlike Wenders's film, Wolf's novel accepts the division of Germany as an incontrovertible fact (perhaps even justifies it as necessary), something the characters will have to live with.

In the context of Berlin's 750th anniversary celebrations Wenders's *Wings of Desire / Der Himmel über Berlin* became an homage to the entire city—for Wenders, the "sky/heaven" above Berlin is not divided, suggesting that on an abstract, spiritual level, the political and ideological divisions on the ground do not exist, that such divisions are quite literally restricted merely to the surface. In the mid-1980s, when Germany was divided politically, this seemed to be a naive and anachronistic stance to take: the city's western half was loosely affiliated with the Bundesrepublik Deutschland (BRD; in English, Federal Republic of Germany or FRG), whereas the city's eastern half had become the capital of communist East Germany, the Deutsche Demokratische Republik (DDR; in English, German Democratic Republic or GDR). In the 1970s, the GDR had attained international recognition as a sovereign state, and it did not look as though things would change any time soon. The Wall that separated the two halves of the city appeared as a physical manifestation of the incontrovertible fact that Cold War divisions were cemented for all eternity. In the West, an insistence on German unity was by and large dismissed as a concern only of marginal reactionary groups or foolhardy nationalistic dreamers with little tangible influence or consequence. At a time when any change to the status quo seemed unlikely, Wenders's film sought to wrest the idea of an overarching unity of the city—and of the German people—from the hands of right-wing political demagogues.

To be sure, Wenders had encountered such supposedly "superficial" divisions as restrictions that were only too real, with East German authorities refusing permission to shoot substantial parts of the film on location in East Berlin. Such practical restrictions are not the only reason why it can be argued that *Wings of Desire* is a kind of simulacrum in which a part is made to stand for the whole: it masquerades as a Berlin film, when it actually is a distinctly *West* Berlin film, reflecting decidedly Western sensibilities. This is all the more remarkable in view of early drafts of the film script: at one point, the film was to open with two helicopter shots, one encircling the Fernsehturm (the TV tower built in the 1960s near East Berlin's Alexanderplatz), the other hovering around the Funkturm (the radio tower built in the 1920s near West Berlin's trade fair grounds).[5] These shots, which were to include observations of everyday activities of ordinary people on either side of the Wall, would have reinforced the idea that, on a significant level, the city remained undivided. One of the places where the angels congregate, in early drafts of the script, was to be on top of the Brandenburg Gate, the city's famous landmark marooned on the eastern side of the Wall.[6] In its final form, however, *Wings of Desire* contains only a few seconds of footage shot in East Berlin, in a brief sequence that shows the angels "walking through" the Wall and exploring drab, largely desolate, streets in East Berlin's Prenzlauer Berg district. The footage was shot clandestinely, without permission, which may explain its brevity. It had to be smuggled across the Wall into West Berlin.

Even while it acknowledges the existence of the eastern part of the city, *Wings of Desire* displays very little interest in engaging with the specific dynamics of life on the other side of the Wall. Despite their ostensibly unencumbered mobility, and their supposedly limitless empathy for the everyday concerns and worries of humans,

Clandestine images of East Berlin.

Wenders's angels for the most part remain firmly on the western side of the Wall. The East appears only in brief glimpses, in the distance behind the Wall, viewed from the West. The angels' mobility contrasts sharply with the fact that to most East Berliners it was precisely the lack of mobility that constituted a sense of discontent: living in the presence of the Wall, an object that could not officially be acknowledged but that could also not be ignored, East Berliners were constantly reminded that they lacked something that their brethren on the other side seemed to have. Viewers familiar with the city will note that Wenders's angels only record the thoughts and concerns of West Berliners. All the locations mentioned in Damiel and Cassiel's conversation in the BMW showroom (itself located on West Berlin's posh Kurfürstendamm) are in the western districts of the city: Kreuzberg (Naunynstraße, Mariannenplatz), Wedding (Virchow Clinic), Charlottenburg (Plötzensee Prison), Schöneberg (Post Office 44, Apostel-Paulus Church), as well as Dahlem, Bahnhof Zoo Station, and the Rehberge park—with a non-existent "Lilienthaler Chaussee" thrown in for good measure.

Likewise, the film shows some well-known West Berlin locations, such as the Kaiser-Wilhelm-Memorial Church, the Stadtautobahn express highway, the angel atop the Siegessäule (Victory Column), the ruins of Anhalter Bahnhof, Güntzelstraße subway station, as well as the rotating Mercedes star on top of the high-rise Europa Center, at the time the commercial hub of West Berlin. Residents of Berlin will also identify other West Berlin locations not specifically named in the film, such as Hallesches Tor in Kreuzberg (with its angel on top of Belle Alliance column, a kind of miniature version of the Siegessäule), the Bunker and the Sozialpalast tenement on Pallas-Straße (where an American film-with-the-film project starring Peter Falk takes place), or Langenscheidt bridge (the site of a motorbike accident), both in Schöneberg.

Even without access to specific locations in the East, references to East Berlin locations would of course have been easy to include in the script, and scenes recording the inner musings of residents of East Berlin apartment buildings would have been easy to simulate in the studio. It would seem, then, that the film in a sense deliberately avoids looking beyond the Wall. It thus displays a decidedly Western perspective, prevalent in West Germany and other countries of the Western world at the time, that unconsciously takes the Western half of the city for the whole, with East Berlin occupying a blind spot: Wenders's angels live on the western side of the Wall, in the magnificent, postmodern structure of the Staatsbibliothek West, designed by star architect Hans Scharoun as a companion to his famous Philharmonie concert hall across the street. The library building turns its back at the Wall, with all public access points on its western side, its design suggesting that the division of the city would last forever.

The implicitly Western bias of the film is also evident in the plot structure: the film seems to suggest that it is only on the western side of the Cold War divide that Damiel-as-human has a future—the possibility of Damiel becoming human on the eastern side of the Wall is never entertained. Nor does the film show any interest in the specific concrete political or ideological dimension of the division of the city. None of the "inner voices" that the angels, and we the audience, overhear address the division as such, including its impact on families that have been separated, or relatives and friends on the other side the Wall that West Berliners are worried about. Neither does the film address forms of grassroots resistance to the Communist dictatorship and democratic reform efforts that emerged in the 1980s in East Germany in the wake of the *Solidarność* movement in Poland or the liberalization of Soviet policies under Mikhail Gorbachev. Instead, it opts for a general, existential perspective that implicitly posits Western values and modalities, including freedom of travel, the prevalence of Anglo-American popular culture, free-market capitalism, and pluralistic liberal democracy, as the unquestioned norm.

And yet, East Berlin *is* present throughout the film, perhaps precisely because it is largely left out. The "other half" of the city functions as a palpable structuring absence. West Berlin's status as an island of Western culture, politics, and commerce surrounded by something ominously "other" is referenced, for instance, when Marion muses, "You can't get lost in Berlin, you always end up at the Wall."[7] Taken literally, this statement seems patently absurd, given that West Berlin stretched across a vast expanse, covering a surface of over 480 square kilometers (nearly 186 square miles). Yet on a deeper, metaphorical level, Marion's statement points to a profound truth: ultimately, people's movements in the Western part of the city are limited and circumscribed by its status as an isolated outpost of Western (capitalist) civilization. As the suicidal man on top of West Berlin's Europa Center high-rise notes when he muses, "which way is East?—Actually, East is all around,"[8] East here does not designate a geographic location but a set of geopolitical Cold War conditions. Under such conditions, a sense of personal autonomy and individual agency is only to be gained by ignoring, or repressing, geopolitical givens.

The skies above Berlin, it seems, resonate mainly, if not exclusively, with Western noises and concerns, indicating Wenders's distinctly Western perspective and positionality. Much of this, it seems, has to do with the particular circumstances surrounding the making of the film. In the mid-1980s, Wenders and his then romantic partner, French actress Solveig Dommartin, who plays Marion in the film, worked on preparing a film project of gigantic proportions, *Till the End of the World* (*Bis ans Ende der Welt*, released in 1991), which was to involve filming in nine countries on five continents. The complicated preparations for this multinational project stalled in 1986, and Wenders decided to take on an interim project, focusing on his new, immediate environment, by making a film about the there and then of his German place of residence, the city of (West) Berlin.

Slow Homecoming: Language and National Identity

Wings of Desire is Wenders's first German film after a long hiatus—mostly spent in the United States—and it marks a new beginning and an effort to reconnect with his German roots. In the late 1970s, following the success of his 1976 film, *Der amerikanische Freund* (*The American Friend*), based on a Patricia Highsmith novel, Wenders had been invited to San Francisco by Francis Ford Coppola, who wanted to set up his Zoetrope studio as an alternative to mainstream Hollywood by recruiting leading non-American directors. Wenders was supposed to direct a detective thriller, *Hammett*, based on the crime novels of Dashiel Hammett. The venture was mired in problems and controversies, since the German director and his American producer did not see eye to eye, resulting in numerous interruptions and rewrites and requiring complicated re-shoots. Quarrels over the final shape of the project dragged on for several years. Wenders vented his frustrations in a deeply personal "interim" film, *Der Stand der Dinge* (*The State of Things*, 1982), shot on Portugal's Atlantic coast. It pits a European art-film director against unscrupulous American producers in a bleak dystopian vision of a film project gone wrong. For this endeavor Wenders enlisted the help of veteran French cinematographer Henri Alekan (1909–2001), who had been responsible, for instance, for the cinematic magic of many of Jean Cocteau's films. *Hammett* was finally released in 1982, in a version that, Wenders felt, did not correspond to his own vision as a filmmaker. Another result of these meager years in the United States was a collaboration with celebrated American playwright Sam Shepard on *Paris, Texas*, which Wenders shot without the support of Coppola or other major American financiers. In 1984, Wim Wenders returned to Germany from his sojourn of more than seven years in America and settled in West Berlin to edit *Paris, Texas*, a project that, like the ones preceding it, had been mired in problems.

Wenders reflected on his near-abortive experience on the periphery of the American studio system in a lengthy prose poem, entitled "The American Dream," written (in English and German) in the spring of 1984. Here, Wenders traces his ambivalent fascination with American popular culture that originated in his youth, noting that comic strips, movies, especially Westerns, and rock 'n' roll signaled freedom and adventure to him. The sense of elation of first arriving "at home" in New York, as a city at once familiar and new, was quickly eroded by the shock of the exploitative inflation of imagery on American television that, in Wenders's view, bears no relation to people's actual experience. American TV, the poem states, offers pre-packaged clichés to "a people / who have forgotten to SEE, / because they've gotten used to / everything BEING SHOWN to them."[9] The proliferation of "empty images," on television and elsewhere, Wenders argues, exerts a "totalitarian" ideological control over people all over the world.[10] More specifically, TV has had a disastrous impact on the art of motion pictures: "after television came to look like permanent advertising, / movies came to look like television."[11] Wenders insists on the need to regain the ability to see, to engage in the world around him without the filter of preconceived categories.

In seeking to answer the question, "What happened to my own American Dream?," Wenders reaches a bleak, pessimistic conclusion: "The 'American Dream' [...] it's been exploited and abused for so long / that now it's nothing more / than a means of exploitation and abuse itself."[12] Viewed in this light, *Wings of Desire*, as Wenders's first film project after his return to Germany, amounts to a kind of stock-taking: what, the film seems to ask, is the state of affairs some four decades after the war in the country that had brought about unprecedented devastation? What does it mean to be German, living at the fault lines of the Cold War division of the world into two power blocs, dominated by the United States in the West and the Soviet Union in the East? Both Germanys had, in a sense, become the poster children for their respective side of the divide: the Federal Republic of Germany, after its "economic miracle" of the 1950s, had become a model satellite of the US; likewise, the German Democratic Republic had excelled at adhering to the hard-line communism of the USSR.

What effects do the problematic legacies of the past and the peculiar conditions of the present have on a sense of German identity? Wenders noted that for the longest time he experienced a "vacuum" when it came to his identity as a German. Upon his return to Germany from the US, it was the German language that provided him with the firmest sense of being German. Applying the German term for shot, frame, or take in a film, "Einstellung" (literally: attitude, positioning, adjustment), Wenders sees language as a means that determines a person's "relation to the world." Settling in West Berlin meant that Wenders had to rediscover and reclaim his native language. In particular, he credits a book by Peter Handke, *Langsame Heimkehr* (*Slow Homecoming*, 1979), itself the story of the return to Europe from the United States of a German-speaking geologist, for helping him reconnect with the language and culture of Germany, in a "movement back into my own language, into my own relation to the world."[13]

The "homecoming" associated with Wenders's return to Germany was "slow," that is, it was a difficult and arduous process that required considerable effort. The city and the country to which he returned, Wenders noted, was "almost totally engulfed in foreign images," images originating in the American entertainment industry. It was American films that dominated on the cinema screens and in video stores. Yet the German language had endured: Wenders emphasized that in his view it is German literature that provided "a counterculture that has not changed and that will not change: the realm of storytelling, reading and writing, the word."[14]

From this perspective, the decision to film in (West) Berlin, in German, to address specifically German issues in a highly poetic, literary, manner and to enlist the help of none other than Peter Handke himself can be read as an effort to counterbalance the alienating effect of the preponderance of pre-fabricated, imported images. The film seeks to reclaim something that is authentic, significant, and unique, both to the (divided) nation as a whole and to the individual person. At the same time, *Wings of Desire* acknowledges that the city is not ethnically homogeneous but populated by people from many countries, highlighted by the various languages heard on the soundtrack—including German, English, French, Turkish, Hebrew, Japanese, even a short bit of Persian.

Significantly, Wenders's focus on language as a unifying characteristic that underpins a sense of German identity elides the differences that existed after decades of political division for Germans on either side of the Iron Curtain. The sky over Berlin is undivided, as is the German language: both Germanys could lay claim, with some legitimacy, to cultural giants like Goethe and Schiller and other figures representing Germany's cultural patrimony, such as Martin

Luther and Gotthold Ephraim Lessing, Heinrich Heine and the German Romantics, Theodor Fontane and Gerhart Hauptmann, the Expressionist poets, Thomas and Heinrich Mann, Bertolt Brecht, as well as Anna Seghers and Christa Wolf. It was this sense of a shared heritage that led protesters in the German Democratic Republic in the famous Monday night demonstrations in 1989 to shift from claiming, "Wir sind das Volk" ("We Are the People"—implying that the country's Communist government was beholden to serving its constituents) to "Wir sind ein Volk" ("We Are One People"), expressing a sense that despite decades of political division Germans had remained a nation that shared a common language, a common history, and common cultural traditions.

To be sure, Wenders acknowledges that West Germany, and to a certain extent even East Germany, had been thoroughly, and largely willingly, Americanized by the "imported pleasures" from the United States following the Second World War.[15] Moreover, his dire assessment in the early 1980s of his sojourn in America and his love/hate relationship with Americana was perhaps overly pessimistic. In fact, *Paris, Texas*, his filmic meditation on the United States that in some ways parallels the ambivalences expressed in the prose poem "The American Dream," was highly successful, garnering him the coveted *Palme d'Or* award for best film at the Cannes Film Festival in 1984. Wenders never fully abandoned his fascination with, and dependence upon, American films and Anglo-American popular culture. He even returned to making films in the United States again, starting with segments for *Till the End of the World* (1991). Other full-length features, including *The End of Violence* (1997), *The Million Dollar Hotel* (1999), *Land of Plenty* (2004), and *Don't Come Knocking* (2005) followed, as well as documentaries, such as the episode *The Soul of a Man* (2004), his contribution to Martin Scorsese's seven-part history of the Blues as an African-American art form, *Blues: A Musical Journey*.

Sites and Sights: Tracing Traumas and Wounds

When Wim Wenders settled in West Berlin in 1984, he actually did not know the city very well himself. Wenders was born in 1945 in Düsseldorf, North-Rhine Westphalia, that is, in the western part of the Federal Republic, and studied at the Film and Television Academy in Munich, in the south German state of Bavaria. He had visited Berlin only sporadically—most notably to shoot parts of his full-length graduation film in 1970, which bears the English title, *Summer in the City*, in homage to the 1960s hit tune by the American band The Lovin' Spoonful. Wenders's decision to move to Berlin in the mid-1980s was thus both a "homecoming" of sorts and a venture into a new place. For Wenders, both gestures were associated with a sense of becoming aware of, and actively embracing, his identity as a German.

In "An Attempted Description of an Indescribable Film," the preface to an early treatment for what would become *Wings of Desire*, Wenders comments that his visits to Berlin had always provided him with a sense of experiencing the "real Germany" because here "history is still present physically and emotionally, unlike elsewhere in 'Germany,' [. . .] where it can only be experienced [. . .] as denial or absence."[16] In other places in West Germany, Wenders argued in a different context, it was easier to avoid confrontations with Germany's problematic Nazi past. Growing up in a climate of denial, Wenders sensed: "Behind us was a black hole, and everybody was staring into the future as if in a trance, busily working on the reconstruction of Germany, on the 'miracle'—and, as I see it, this economic miracle was only possible through a gigantic act of repression."[17]

The motif of active repression and denial of a troublesome political history appears in an early draft of the script to *Wings of Desire*: the main conceit of angels watching over the city was to be complemented by a more sinister presence: a group of die-hard *Werwölfe* (werewolves), youngsters recruited into the Nazi army in the final stages of the Second World War, were supposed to be still living in an underground hideout some four decades after the end of the war, waiting for the right moment to re-emerge to the surface. Now grown men in their late fifties, they were preparing to take control of the city. In their refusal to accept fundamentally changed new realities, they were to cause considerable trouble for angel Cassiel, who seeks to keep them in check, suggesting that Berlin in the 1980s was still a city haunted by demons from its Nazi past. This politically charged narrative strand of a potential neo-fascist dirty underbelly in Berlin was eliminated as the film project shifted towards a more abstract reflection of the burdens associated with Germany's history.

If the United States, as the prose poem "The American Dream" claims, is the country where everything is fake, where exploitative, commercial images render authentic experience impossible, Berlin (again, we have to note that the reference is primarily to the Western part of the city) to Wenders appears as a place where an engagement with what is real, tangible, and authentic, is possible and necessary. Berlin bears the visible scars of the past, evidence of the devastation and destruction wrought by German history: empty lots where buildings used to be, and ruins such as the steeple of the Kaiser-Wilhelm-Memorial Church and the remnants of the entrance hall of Anhalter Station serve as reminders of the aerial bombings that reduced much of the city to rubble; bullet holes still visible in the decaying facades of old apartment buildings attest to the street fighting when the Soviet army entered the city in 1945.

Between 1961 and 1989, the most prominent scar that acted as a tangible reminder of the tragic derailments of German history was the Berlin Wall. The term "Wall," suggesting a single barrier, is a misnomer of sorts, since the border between East and West Berlin consisted of an elaborate and intricate system of various fortifications. It comprised several layers: facing the West, there was a wall indicating the borders of East German territory—the surfaces of which provided ample opportunities for spray-paint artists and writers of polemical graffiti. (*Wings of Desire* features a brief glimpse of French street artist Thierry Noir, who is shown on a ladder painting the Wall on Waldemarstraße in West Berlin's Kreuzberg district near where Damiel finds himself after he has turned human.) Facing the East, another wall prevented people from coming near the border zone. In between, there was the so-called "Death Strip," framed by a system of barbed wire electrified fences with sensors that triggered shooting devices. This strip of land itself contained elaborate sets of booby traps and land-mines that would blow up anyone who stepped on them. The pristine whiteness of the walls on either side of this terrain indicated that it was out of reach for the citizens of East Germany. Euphemistically termed by East German authorities an *antifaschistischer Schutzwall* ("anti-fascist protective wall"), it was officially designed to keep alleged Western imperialist agitators from entering the country. From a Western perspective, the Wall curtailed the freedom of movement and travel of East German citizens, turning the East German dictatorship into a prison of sorts.

The Wall figures as a tangible presence in *Wings of Desire*, even if its direct impact upon the lives of Berliners East and West is hardly ever touched upon: in the din of radio voices surrounding the West Berlin Funkturm at the beginning of the film, there is mention of traffic congestion at the *Kontrollpunkte*, the checkpoint exits in the Wall that allowed West Berliners to travel, through East German territory, to destinations beyond the city. And, in his conversation with Cassiel in the BMW showroom, Damiel briefly references a recent attempt by Easterners to cross the Wall by way of a hot air balloon. Besides such casual references, the Wall is treated by the film simply as a given, as a special condition of life in the divided city. The Wall was a visible and inescapable reminder of the burden of Germany's violent twentieth-century past. Elsewhere in Germany, much of the devastation wrought by the Second World War was glossed over by a veneer of business and efficiency. By way of contrast,

The (simulated) "Death Strip" of the Berlin Wall.

the city of Berlin, Wenders quotes from an exhibition catalog, is an "historical site of truth," adding: "Berlin is more real than any other city. Just that: a SITE, rather than a CITY."[18]

The quest for authenticity takes two forms in *Wings of Desire*. On the one hand, it involves an effort to "see," that is, to pay attention to the world by registering and recording experiences and to collect authentic images that are not pre-packaged or pre-digested by commercial mass media. On the other hand, it pertains to an engagement with issues of national identity and questions of ethics: given the burden of twentieth-century history, what does it mean to be German? The city Wenders depicts in this film is pockmarked with reminders of the destruction of the Second World War that refuse to go away, such as the many empty lots between apartment buildings flanked by bare firewalls, the high-rise bunker that serves as the location for the shooting of the American movie project and the bunker near Anhalter Bahnhof that bears the ominous inscription, "Wer Bunker baut, wirft Bomben" (He who builds bunkers drops

"He who builds bunkers throws bombs."

bombs).[19] Visually, the past repeatedly comes alive in the film by way of the historic documentary footage edited into the main narrative—including aerial bombardments, people running from burning buildings, dead bodies lined up on the street, and the burnt-out husks of apartment buildings whose outer walls have been blown away. How can a productive sense of national identity be forged from the cauldron of the multiple catastrophes we associate with twentieth-century German history?

Berlin, Wenders argues, afforded him with an opportunity to address questions raised by his sojourn in the United States, a country consumed by its own simulacrum, where the fakeness of the "American Dream" had rendered it impossible to know "how to live." If Berlin is a site in which authentic experience is possible, it is a place that potentially allows answers to what Wenders calls "the only and persistent question: How is one to live?"[20] To Wenders, then, the question of national identity ("who am I?") is inextricably linked with that of individual identity. It is Marion, the trapeze artist, who will articulate this question in the film itself, when she asks, in French: "How am I to live?"[21]

Few films address such fundamental existential issues with such directness. It would appear then that *Wings of Desire* resonates with audiences, both domestic and international, to a large part on account of these dynamics. The film seeks to address, for the German viewer, national issues of history, ethics, and identity, while it also invites international audiences to contemplate these interrelated issues from a global perspective. Perhaps more than any of Wenders's other films, *Wings of Desire* makes good on what Michael Corvino has noted as the distinguishing feature of many of Wenders's early films, that they convey "a sense of things [...] that somehow corresponds to what our own nerves tell us about the world."[22] The power of *Wings of Desire*, for many viewers, rests in the sense that the film addresses existential concerns that are acute and real.

Starting Over: Childhood, Seeing, and Writing

What do "our own nerves tell us about the world" in this film? The first thing we see at the beginning of *Wings of Desire* is an extreme close-up in black-and-white of a male hand writing with an ink pen on a piece of paper. A male voice—which we will later discover is the voice of the angel Damiel—recites the same lines that we see being written: "When the Child was a Child." The poem, written by Peter Handke, will reoccur several times in the film. As it continues, the voice changes into a kind of sing-song, reminiscent of a children's song or nursery rhyme:

> When the child was a child, it walked with its arms swinging.
> It wanted the stream to be a river, the river a torrent ... and
>   this puddle to be the sea.
> When the child was a child, it didn't know it was a child.
> Everything was full of life, and all life was one.

Damiel's hand writing "The Song of Childhood."

> When the child was a child, it had no opinion about
>   anything.
> It had no habits. It often sat cross-legged, took off running
>   . . .
> had a cowlick in its hair, and didn't pull a face . . . when
>   photographed.

Right at the beginning, then, several themes are introduced that
will resonate later on. First of all, there is the motif of childhood
as a state of being characterized by a lack of self-awareness or
self-consciousness. Here, the film is indebted to the idealization
of childhood in German Romanticism, and the fairy tales of the
Brothers Grimm, E. T. A. Hoffmann, and Wilhelm Hauff. As
Charles H. Helmetag has pointed out, Handke's poem echoes
passages in the Bible, notably 1 Corinthians 13: 11–12.[23] The concept
of a mode of existence that precedes individuation will later occur in
the musings of the old man identified in the script as Homer, who
calls it *Kindschaft*—childhood, "childness," or as the English subtitles
of the film's 4K re-release have it, "childship"—not in the sense of

a specific period in a person's life, but as a disposition of openness toward the world. To a "child" in this sense, the world is "full of life," or, as the German original has it, "beseelt"—animated, full of soul. Moreover, it is a state where judgment or conceptual distinctions do not (yet) exist, or are suspended—"all life was one"; in German, "alle Seelen waren ihm eins" (to the child, all souls were one). "Childship," as an attentive mode of experience that is open to the world, without interpreting or passing judgment, is combined with writing, as a means of recording observations and preserving memories.

The film's opening lines run the risk of reverting to worn-out Romantic clichés idealizing childhood as a prelapsarian state of supposed innocence. This tendency is counterbalanced when the poem makes its second appearance: as Damiel recites the poem's second stanza, we see a group of children excitedly playing video games in a cramped room. Perhaps their video game is the modern equivalent of the venture into imaginary worlds we associate with German Romanticism. Yet these children seem to show little interest in the lofty existential questions raised in this stanza: "When the child was a child, it was the time of these questions: Why am I me, and why not you? Why am I here, and why not there? When did time begin, and where does space end?"[24]

The hand we see and the voice we hear at the beginning of the film make claims about the nature of things. What may be mere personal observations are presented as incontrovertible givens. (Interestingly enough, in Handke's notebook the poem was initially in the first person, "When I was a Child," and was changed later into a more general statement).[25] We viewers don't as yet know whose hand we are seeing or whose voice we are hearing, and we have no way of vouching for the authority of these pronouncements. Moreover, there are many strange tensions associated with this opening shot: for instance, the shift towards sing-song of the as-yet-disembodied adult voice turns a somewhat philosophical reflection into a quasi-nursery rhyme, suggesting that the speaker himself here enters into a childlike state, performing the gesture of letting go of an "adult" mode of communication. At the same time, the extreme close-up of the hand with the fountain pen moving across a piece of paper subtly aligns us viewers with the writer/speaker/singer, whose perspective we immediately come to share, much as if we ourselves were writing the words we hear. Is it we ourselves who utter these statements and write them down on paper? Viewers are put in a position of suspended judgment, of having to wait to make sense of this image and of the ones that follow.

Throughout this sequence, the film introduces a subtle tension between what we see and what we hear: while the sing-song voice recites several lines of the poem, the hand we see only manages to complete little more than the key phrase, "When the child was a child, it didn't know it was a child." The voice utters more words than appear on the screen, alerting us to the disjunction between speaking and writing, as processes that proceed at different speeds. The physical act of writing takes longer than the act of speaking: there is a disjuncture between the visual and the audio register of the film, a characteristic that will continue later on, where dissolves mark the transition between shots and audio-bridges serve to connect images before and beyond their appearance on screen. Such techniques require an active viewership, since we are constantly asked to reflect on the links that hold together the various images and sounds we encounter.

What follows is a sequence of frames that list the main credits, inscribed in rough, upper-case letters as if written in chalk on a school blackboard. Within a few seconds, the film thus reinforces the childhood/childship motif by visually referencing schooling and learning, suggesting a connection between the film and starting anew. The film's title emerges at the end of this brief sequence, dissolving into a shot of a cloudy sky. Here, the difference between the international release title of the film, *Wings of Desire*, and the original German title, *Der Himmel über Berlin* ("the sky/heaven over Berlin"), begins to matter: we see images of a cloudy sky that,

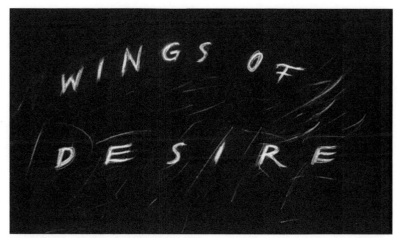

The film's title—chalk on a blackboard.

we may assume, is that above the city of Berlin, a specific reference not evoked by the more generic English title that connotes a vague notion of "desire" with its metaphorical "wings." A cut reveals a brief extreme close-up of an eye, presumably of a male, that directly gazes into the camera. This gaze, we will soon learn, will align the viewer with the view of the angels, an all-seeing gaze that appears not to be subject to limitations of any kind. The eye dissolves into aerial shots of rooftops, subtly blending, for a few brief moments, subject (observer) and object (the terrain viewed), with the camera hovering above the nested courtyards typical of traditional nineteenth- and early twentieth-century Berlin apartment buildings. Cut to a person with angel wings standing high on a ledge against an as-yet undefined city background. As the wings fade away, there is an abrupt cut to an extreme high-angle shot of pedestrians crossing a city street on a crosswalk, seen from the angel's point of view. A child stops, blocking the flow of traffic, looking up. Cut to a low-angle shot, from the child's point of view, of the steeple of Kaiser-Wilhelm-Memorial Church, a church left in ruins after the war, as a reminder

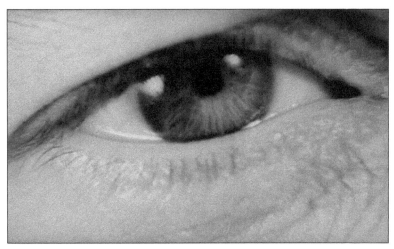

The all-seeing angel's / camera's eye.

of the devastation brought to Berlin. We can make out the outlines of a presence on top of the steeple, with wings, like a bird or an angel figure. The unusual angles of these shots reveal that they are point-of-view shots from the perspective of the personages shown: like the angel, we viewers first look down upon the city street; and, like the child, we then look up to the top of the church steeple. Gradually it is revealed that in the fictional world of the film only children can "see" the angels. We as viewers are thus thematically aligned in multiple ways with the film's personages: like the children, we can see the angels, too. This alignment is underscored by the way in which the film visually pulls the viewers in, by way of point-of-view shots, to become part of the filmic experience.

The opening shots establish the visual logic of the film, which is characterized by what Wenders calls a "loving gaze." This gaze includes the viewer as well as the personages and events that occur in the fictional world we encounter, and it is a visual mode that is both compassionate and non-judgmental, seeming merely to register

A child stops to look up to Damiel, from his point of view.

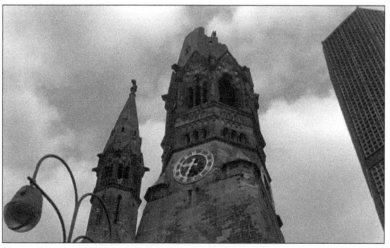

The angel, on top of Memorial Church, from the child's point of view.

things and events as they occur. Time and again, the beginning of the film shows children looking upward to something outside the frame, followed by a matching shot of the sky: the attention of an infant strapped to the back of a man walking on a street is drawn to a lone bird crossing the sky; from its seat behind a young woman on a bicycle, a child looks up at an airplane. An overall mood of melancholy is enhanced by the music that accompanies these images: we hear disjointed notes plucked on a string instrument, reminiscent of a cerebral, modernist avant-garde composition. Gradually a mournful melody emerges, played on a cello. Thus far, it has been impossible for the viewer to make much sense of the sequence of seemingly unrelated images. This changes with a quick transition from the child looking at a plane to placing us inside the plane, where we will meet the American star, Peter Falk, on his way to Berlin.

As the camera pans along the inside aisle past the rows of passengers in the plane, the visual logic of the film is subtly reinforced when a blonde girl, drawing with her crayons, smiles at Damiel. Shown from Damiel's point of view, she looks directly at the camera, thus smiling not only at him, but at us viewers as well; and, returning her gaze, shown from her point of view, Damiel also smiles at us. More such moments occur later on, for instance, with two girls looking up from inside a bus, with an isolated boy on the playground, or with the handicapped girl in the apartment building. The opening shots of the film thus continuously violate one of the cardinal rules of conventional cinema, which stipulates that we are shown on-screen spaces as if a "fourth wall" were removed, and that on-screen characters do not acknowledge the presence of the camera as a recording apparatus.

The technique that pulls the viewer into the fictional world of a film is called "suturing" in film studies parlance. Normally, such suturing is restricted to placing the viewer momentarily in the position of one of the characters by way of a point-of-view shot. Here, however, the viewer is also repeatedly addressed as an

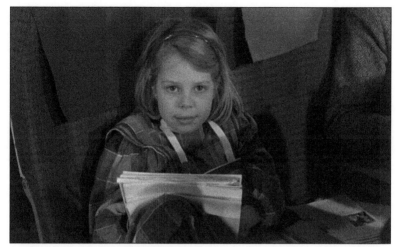

A girl on the plane looks at Damiel / the camera / us.

Damiel smiling at the girl / the camera / us.

active participant in the unfolding of the story. Damiel—and, on occasion, other characters—directly look at us through the camera, in violation of the standard "fourth wall" rule. Visually, the film thus becomes as much "about us" as viewers as it is about the fictional characters we see on screen. Viewers constantly oscillate between four subject positions: we are omniscient observers of the fictional world we encounter (very much in keeping with how mainstream films work), and we are pulled into the fictional world itself—as addressees of the filmic presentation, as well as by adopting the children's or the angels' points of view.

Engaging the Viewer: A "Loving Gaze"

Wings of Desire is dedicated in the closing credits to three "former angels," filmmakers Yasujirō Ozu (1903–63), François Truffaut (1932–84), and Andrej Tarkovsky (1932986). This suggests that Wenders in his film sought to emulate key characteristics of these director's respective styles, as noted by critic Linda C. Ehrlich:

> Traces of all three directors are apparent in *Wings of Desire*: Ozu's glorification of the simple moments of life, with all of their reverberations; Truffaut's portrayal of children as spiritual vessels, and his *Fahrenheit 451* in which people represent books they have memorized; Tarkovsky's transcendental black and white *mise-en-scène*.[26]

Time and again, by looking at the camera, the film's characters also look at us, the viewers, and we become the implicit addressees of the "loving gaze" that permeates the film. The camera draws our attention to things we tend hardly to notice in regular life, either because they take place where we can't see them or because we find them too insignificant to register. Likewise, by letting us hear the thoughts of West Berlin's residents, in a variety of languages, the soundtrack provides us with access to the minds of fellow human beings, something to which we are not normally privy. *Wings of Desire* asks us to acknowledge things we normally overlook or cannot access, to watch and listen with attentiveness and compassion. As viewers, we become partners in an active, communicative exchange different from the regular viewing experience that treats viewers by and large as passive recipients of filmic images. The collage of short vignettes that opens the film involves each viewer in the construction of his or her own film—and every viewer will interpret the various short segments according to his or her own personal thoughts and associations.

Given Wenders's distrust of television as an instrument of mass deception, one shot is particularly strange: we see an elderly man mindlessly staring ahead of himself as he muses about what will become of his estranged son. With a quick cut, a reverse shot is introduced that shows that the man is gazing at his television set, revealing that the previous perspective was, as it were, from "within" the television set. The film thus turns the traditional shot/reverse shot technique into an ambivalent critique of television as a kind of surveillance instrument but also as the locus from which we, the viewers, see the scene, suggesting that, try as we may, we are all inescapably implicated in the networks of image-producing media. It is significant that the American "film star," Peter Falk, is actually best known internationally for his work on television, the mass cultural media Wenders excoriates in his prose poem "The American Dream" as responsible for the hollowing out of perception. At various points in the film, Falk is associated with his most famous TV persona, the bumbling detective Columbo, from the eponymous TV series that ran for seven seasons in the 1970s (and that would, in 1989, be revived for two more seasons as well as a few specials). In *Wings of Desire*, Falk's character later turns out to be a former angel himself, who has come to Berlin to star in an American film production, playing an American detective searching for a German

man during the final, chaotic stages of Nazi Germany, in an unlikely plot that Falk himself calls "dopey." Even a former angel, it seems, is inextricably tied up in the contradictions and tensions surrounding the production of images.

Falk's thoughts as he approaches the city in an airplane meander from the threadbare American movie script that he attempts to read (with little interest) to the city itself. He associates the city with John F. Kennedy (presumably, the famous visit of 1963), Emil Jannings (the emblematic actor, representing German film history), and General von Stauffenberg (the head of a conspiracy of German officers in 1944 to assassinate Hitler). In deadpan fashion, Falk praises Stauffenberg as a "hell of a guy," while noting that the attempted coup did not actually take place in Berlin itself. We hear the first subtle hints of a possible biographical connection between Falk's character and the German city, "If Grandma was here, she'd say: 'Spazieren . . . Go spazieren!'" Falk then seems to reflect on the interconnectedness of global cities, by listing a series of locations that, we have to assume, he has visited at some point: "Tokyo, Kyoto, Paris, London, Trieste—Berlin."[27] Upon the word "Berlin," the soundtrack of the film changes dramatically: the din of indistinct human voices morphs into an orchestral score over which a haunting cello melody hovers, the music begins to soar, signaling that the film proper has now begun.

Throughout the first third of the film, *Wings of Desire* offers a collage of seemingly unrelated shots difficult for audiences to interpret, while playing with the fact that we cannot *not* (attempt to) interpret what we see. For instance, in a film about Berlin that begins with aerial shots, we may expect to see images of the Wall that divides the city into two unequal halves representing two different political systems. Yet instead of views of this infamous Cold War edifice, we see different types of divisions, divisions that exist within the western part of the city. The camera hovers above the Stadtautobahn, the express highway at the western edge of downtown West Berlin,

The old man, seen from "within" his TV set.

The "film star" Peter Falk, musing about Berlin.

lined with noise-cancelling walls and control towers that eerily resemble the Wall we associate with the city. We see the Congress Centrum, a gigantic postmodern building complex that used to hold international trade fairs and conventions, sitting like a sprawling reptile next to the expressway, a kind of monster of capitalist commerce. Other dividing lines appear, in the shape of Berlin's famous nested inner courtyards surrounded by apartment blocks, a maze of spaces normally hidden from street view. The camera zeros in on the exterior wall of an apartment building and "enters" through the window, as if there were no obstacle. The camera, it seems, is not subject to normal physical, architectural, or political divisions, as it freely floats above and around city space, very much like we might imagine the gaze of angels. The mobile camera of Henri Alekan not only repeatedly ignores cinematic conventions, by breaking the "fourth wall rule," but also by freely moving in and out of spaces as it records vignettes from the everyday lives of various, anonymous (West-)Berliners. The connection between the mobile camera and the unencumbered gaze of angels is clearly inspired by the poetry of Rainer Maria Rilke, who developed a kind of mythology of angels as transcendental "onlookers." Wenders kept quotations from Rilke's poetry on the drawing board of his office while working on the film, and an early draft script prominently features lines from Rilke's eighth *Duino Elegy* on angels as "onlookers" (Zuschauer) as its motto: "Und wir, Zuschauer, immer überall, / dem allen zugewandt und nie hinaus!" (And we: onlookers, always, everywhere, / always looking into, never out of, everything).[28]

The motif of the single eye at the opening of the film hints at a basic ambiguity: reminiscent of the "divine eye" (to be found, for instance, in Masonic symbolism and on American dollar bills), the eye stands for a way of looking that is both transcendent and inherently deficient. The eye's gaze transcends normal limitations of time and space in that it seems to be able to move freely wherever it chooses to go, yet it is also incapable of capturing the fullness of actual

West Berlin, divided by the Stadtbautobahn expressway.

life, lacking both color and volume. To view the world in color and in three dimensions, we later find out, requires a set of eyes within a body. Thus, the film's black-and-white opening anticipates Damiel's quest for a corporeal self that will become the main storyline.

What does this angelic eye see? The filmic apparatus and the angels bear witness to the lives of (West) Berliners by way of listening in on their intimate thoughts, which we hear as changing voiceovers, and by observing them in their everyday environment. The predominant note captured in Henri Alekan's elegantly moving, beautifully composed black-and-white shots, underscored by Jürgen Knieper's eerily ethereal sound score composed of multiple, mostly indistinct voices, is one of profound melancholic listlessness. Every person, it seems, is caught up in their own private world. Later in the film, the impression is reinforced by a voiceover of the limousine chauffeur, a man who theorizes that, in a sense, every German is his or her own sovereign state, surrounded by metaphorical borders that they don't allow others to cross. Even beyond the division of their country, Germans, the film suggests, miss genuine human connections, they lack community. The Cold War division of the city, and of Germany, is thus paralleled on a microcosmic level by the extreme alienation felt by Germans. Berlin, as Wenders put it, is emblematic of an overall situation of modernity: "Berlin is split, just like our world is, just like our times are, and just like each of our experiences."[29] The Wall, it would appear from this perspective, is merely a physical manifestation of the existential isolation felt by each individual.

Yet even as the camera records the preoccupations and concerns of ordinary (West) Berliners, it refrains from passing judgement. The vignettes are too short and devoid of context to enable viewers to determine the exact nature of each experience recorded. The very act of paying attention to the minutiae of everyday life, of bearing witness, amounts to an act of caring. Normally, such everyday events are not regarded as worthy of being recorded, let alone of being highlighted in a feature film. By connecting moments that are normally disregarded or overlooked, the "loving gaze" reaches out to its viewer, contributing towards establishing community: first and foremost, community between screen and audience.

The first gesture that indicates Damiel's interest in joining the world of humans is associated with the act of writing: as he strolls through the Staatsbibliothek, he "picks up" a pencil (the double exposure photography shows the actual pencil remaining on the desk) and twirls it around in his fingers, lost in thought. As he sits down on a chair on a landing of a staircase, he places the virtual pencil on his lap, spreads his arms, holding on to the railing behind him, and slightly tilts his head sideways, assuming a pose reminiscent of depictions of Christ on the cross. Like Christ, the image suggests, Damiel will become human and he will suffer. The placement of the pencil across his crotch suggests a connection between writing and

Damiel in the library, adopting a Christ-like pose.

Damiel's sexuality as a human. To live, to love, to attend to the world and record experience in writing, can involve the vexations of corporal desire as well as a kind of martyrdom. The religious connotations of Damiel's pose are quickly dispelled as another writer, the old man identified in the published script as Homer, slowly ascends the stairs and later sits down in the same spot on the same chair. After a brief slapstick-like struggle with his eyeglasses, the old man firmly grasps the top of his cane with his gnarly hands and confidently looks around: he may be old and exhausted, but there is not a trace of self-pity in his dedication to writerly attentiveness. His pose recalls the famous 1913 portrait by Expressionist painter Ludwig Meidner of Max Herrmann-Neiße (Art Institute of Chicago), the German-Jewish poet who, like countless others, was forced into exile in 1933—a first subtle hint that reinforces the association between the unnamed character of Homer (played by German-Jewish actor Curt Bois) and German-Jewish history.

Homer in the library, surveying the terrain.

Friendship and Bonding: A Transcendental "Buddy Movie"

In many ways, *Wings of Desire* is a paean to male friendship, both on screen and off. The on-screen chemistry between the actors who portray the angels, Bruno Ganz (Damiel) and Otto Sander (Cassiel), owes a lot to the fact that the two had worked together as members of the famed West Berlin Schaubühne theater ensemble under director Peter Stein, first located at the Hallesches Ufer (1970–81), then at Lehniner Platz (1981–85), where they appeared together in numerous productions. In the early 1980s, Ganz and Sander created a documentary film, *Gedächtnis* (*Remembrance*, 1981), an homage to two major twentieth-century German actors—Curt Bois (who would later appear as Homer in *Wings of Desire*) and Bernhard Minetti (who, unlike Bois, did not go into exile during the Third Reich). However, the two had never appeared on screen together as actors before *Wings of Desire*. Much of the relaxed playfulness and easy-going banter that characterizes the dialogs of the angels is attributable to the sense of trust and familiarity that had evolved between these two leading actors after decades of working together. Many of Wenders's early films feature instances of male bonding, most notably the friendship that emerges between Bruno Winter (Rüdiger Vogler) and Robert Lander (Hanns Zischler) in *Im Lauf der Zeit* (*Kings of the Road*, 1975) or the fraught relationship between Jonathan Zimmerman (Bruno Ganz) and Tom Ripley (Dennis Hopper) in *The American Friend* (1976). In both instances, Wenders offered his own complex, often somewhat sinister, take on the genre of the "buddy movie." The friendship between the two angels Damiel and Cassiel in *Wings of Desire* signals a more optimistic perspective on the possibility of human connection. In an interview, Wenders jokingly referred to *Wings of Desire* as a "vertical road movie."[30]

Perhaps most significantly, *Wings of Desire* is the product of the friendship between German filmmaker Wim Wenders and Austrian author Peter Handke. The two men bonded in the mid-1960s, after Wenders attended a performance of Handke's play, *Publikumsbeschimpfung* (*Offending the Audience*, 1966) in the West German city Oberhausen in 1966. While Wenders was still a student at the Munich Film and Television academy, the two collaborated on a short experimental film, *3 amerikanische LP's* (*Three American LP's*, 1969), a mini "road movie" of sorts featuring the music of Credence Clearwater Revival, Harvey Mandel, and Van Morrison. The film attests to their common, ambivalent fascination with Anglo-American pop culture, including jukeboxes, pinball machines, comic strips, and American movies. Wenders based his first commercially distributed feature film, an oblique homage to "film noir" conventions, *Die Angst des Torwarts beim Elfmeter* (*The Goalie's Anxiety at the Penalty Kick*, 1971) on Handke's novel of the same title. Handke later provided the screenplay for Wenders's *Falsche Bewegung* (*Wrong Move*, 1975), and Wenders produced Handke's first major effort as a film director, *Die linkshändige Frau* (*The Left-Handed Woman*, 1976). The friendship between the two continued even during Wenders's

Damiel and Cassiel, debriefing in the BMW showroom.

sojourn in the United States: Wenders directed a stage version of Handke's "dramatic poem" *Über die Dörfer* (*Across the Villages*, 1981) at the Salzburg Festival in August 1982. When, after his return to Germany, Wenders faced problems with the dramatic structure of the project that would become *Wings of Desire* it was thus natural for him to turn to his old friend and to enlist Handke's help for his first "domestic" project in about a decade.

The collaboration between the two artists continued afterwards, with Wenders co-producing another film Handke directed, in France, *L'Absence* (*The Absence*, 1992) and, more recently, directing another French-language film, *Les beaux jours d'Aranjuez* (*The Beautiful Days of Aranjuez*), based on Handke's play *Die schönen Tage von Aranjuez* (2012). Nick Cave, who with his band, The Bad Seeds, had appeared in *Wings of Desire*, makes a surprise on-screen solo appearance at the piano in this film, which premiered at the Venice International Film Festival on September 1, 2016. The love song he performs here, "Into My Arms," pays oblique homage to *Wings of Desire*: "I don't believe in the existence of angels / but looking at you, I wonder if that's true."

Wenders visited Handke in Salzburg in the summer of 1986, asking for help with the project that was to become *Wings of Desire*. Handke felt he was unable to provide a full screenplay, but he agreed to contribute text passages that would fill some of the gaps in Wenders's as-yet-incomplete concept: Handke wrote the text for the three major conversations between Damiel and Cassiel—in the BMW showroom; near a canal in Kreuzberg (originally, this conversation between the two angels was to take place on the Quadriga on top of East Berlin's Brandenburg Gate); and on the "Death Strip" of the Berlin Wall. He also contributed the poem "Lied vom Kindsein" ("Song of Childhood") which permeates the film as a kind of leitmotif, and the "Anrufung des Lebens" ("Invocation of Life") that is recited by the dying man after the motorbike accident. Additionally, Handke supplied Marion's long soliloquy when she finally encounters Damiel in human form in the bar of the Esplanade, as well as Damiel's musings about his first night with Marion that culminate in the phrase, "I now know what no angel knows."[31] Much of this material was incorporated into the film with only minor changes and cuts and slight adjustments of context.

The most significant differences between Handke and Wenders revolved around two clusters of texts: the texts associated with the nameless character who appears as Homer in the printed version of the final script and an extended soliloquy originally intended for Cassiel, whose transformation into a human was also to be told in the film, as a kind of negative foil to that of Damiel. Wenders seems to have initially conceived of an "Angel of Narration" (Engel der Erzählung), as a senior colleague of Damiel and Cassiel named Raphael. Handke proposed to associate the issue of narration with Homer, who as the author of the Greek epics *The Iliad* and *The Odyssey*, is a kind of founding father of Western storytelling.[32] Handke envisioned three major scenes with Homer, all set in a library and based on a painting by Rembrandt that depicts the ancient storyteller: first, he was supposed to be surrounded by a circle of listeners, then only by one listener—a draft version of the script identifies Cassiel as this listener—and finally alone, speaking into the void. After turning human, Cassiel was supposed to have been gripped by despair and to have turned to preaching on street corners, with Handke supplying a lengthy "Predigt des wahnsinnig gewordenen Cassiel kreuz und quer durch die Stadt" (Sermon by Cassiel Gone Insane Criss-Crossing Around Town). As the plans to include Cassiel's experiences as a human were dropped in an effort to wrap up the sprawling film project, these paranoiac rantings were excised, with some isolated phrases repurposed to appear sprinkled into the various inner monologs of the random people the angels encounter in the film, such as the passengers in the subway train. Handke's voice is also present more indirectly—some of Marion's musings are taken from his journal, *Das Gewicht der Welt* (*The Weight of the World*, 1977). Handke's input into the film may indeed have been limited in terms of quantity, yet his contributions are crucial thematically, and they determine much of the overall tone: *Wings of Desire* is characterized by a preponderance of heightened, poetic language that addresses existential and spiritual concerns. Another noted script writer, Richard Reitinger, receives credit for his help in story editing and selecting which particular episodes out of the many that were planned made it into the final version of the film.

Angels and Children: To Take Off Running

In many ways, actors and characters in *Wings of Desire* tend to blend into one another because aspects of the actors' respective biographies are incorporated into the personages they portray on screen. For instance, the character of Marion has much to do with the actress who plays her, Solveig Dommartin, who was Wenders's romantic partner at the time. Marion is the object of desire for angel Damiel, but she is also respected as a subject in her own right, since her trailer is decorated with postcards and mementos related to Dommartin's actual background, attesting to her growing up in Nancy, France. Likewise, the Swiss background of actor Bruno Ganz is subtly referenced by showing his hand writing the text of the "Song of Childhood" using the double-s ("ss"), a Swiss idiosyncrasy—in the standard German of the time, before the various spelling reforms of the 1990s, one would have used the *scharfes s* ("ß"). He also slips into his Swiss accent upon turning human: as Damiel picks up his armor and starts to explore his new existence, Ganz says "Geh' mer!" (a Swiss, as well as South German, version of "Gehen wir"—"Let's get going"). And, as I will show later, much of the background of the Homer character is taken from the actual biography of the actor who plays him, Curt Bois. Perhaps the most extensive, and the most playful, blending of actor and character is that of Peter Falk, who in many ways plays "himself," with refreshingly self-deprecating Jewish humor, as a genial, understated professional screen actor fond of cigarettes, coffee, and sketching during breaks in shooting, as well as his public persona as the streetwise "Columbo," the TV detective that made him famous with international audiences.

In his audio commentaries to the German and the international DVD release of the film, Wenders is apologetic about what he considers an inconsistency in the character of Peter Falk: on the one hand, he is revealed to be a former angel, on the other, we hear him reminisce about advice his grandmother once gave him. As eternal beings, Wenders notes, angels of course don't have a personal past, and thus can't have grandmothers. Yet on another level, such a discrepancy is no more noteworthy than many other issues raised by the film's basic conceit. While watching the film, we viewers don't necessarily take the angelic conceit literally by asking practical questions such as: Why, if angels are dispassionate observers, do they experience and display emotions? How, if angels have no bodies, are they capable of experiencing erotic desire; why do they have a gender; why do they wear coats; and what's up with their funny ponytails? The poetic allure of Wenders's cinematic fairytale renders such mundane questions moot. If angels are capable of becoming human by attaining physical form as a person, that may very well include attaining a personal past as well. In fact, the apparent inconsistency makes Peter Falk's character all the more poignant: Falk's self-deprecating American-Jewish mannerisms attain greater depth by way of giving him a German-Jewish grandmother (with her admonitions of "Go spazieren!"), a gesture that ties Falk's character more closely to Berlin's traumatic history and issues of remembrance. As viewers, we quickly accept that in the fictional world of this film, as in the stories of German Romanticism, anything is possible. Within the fairy-tale world of the film, Wenders has absolute authority over what can and cannot happen; he sets up and controls the rules of the game.

Wenders's film attempts to strike a delicate balance between seriousness (with fundamental existential issues being addressed in an often lofty manner) and comic relief (with episodes that undercut the potential portentousness of Handke's prose). In fact, Wenders had originally conceived of the film as a comedy.[33] For instance, the film plays with the notion of the angels' omniscience when Damiel responds to a Turkish German boy who respectfully asks directions to nearby Akazienstraße. The poor youngster receives an earful of overly detailed instructions, attesting both to Damiel's superior knowledge of the city's topography (presumably, attained through centuries of witnessing the development of the city) and his lack of social skills: not only does he use colloquial forms of the street names ("Potse" for Potsdamer Straße) inappropriate for the interaction of an adult with a young child, but he bombards the boy with a lot of unnecessary detail that renders his information all but useless—small wonder then that the boy turns away exasperated, sighing "Aw, man."[34] He obviously regrets having asked for directions in the first place.

Wenders is also fond of playing with his audiences in other, strictly visual ways, for instance when shots in his films directly "quote" well-known images. Famous cases of such visual quotations include the ending of *Wrong Move*, where aspiring writer Wilhelm (Rüdiger Vogler) stands on the top of Zugspitze mountain with his back to the camera in a pose reminiscent of the famous *Wanderer above the Sea of Fog* (1818) by German Romantic painter Caspar David Friedrich, or shots of an American bar late at night from *The End of Violence* (1997) that pay homage to Edward Hopper's famous painting of urban isolation *Nighthawks* (1942) by restaging that image. Sometimes such visual playfulness is subtle and meaningful, for instance at the end of *Kings of the Road* (1975), where the camera comes to rest on the broken light display of a defunct cinema called "Weiße Wand" (blank wall—the German equivalent of "silver screen"). Only the first two letters, "WW," are illuminated, providing both a commentary on a screen left blank, a wall literally remaining white, and a kind of signing off of the filmmaker, Wim Wenders, since it is his initials that appear in the image. One such moment occurs in *Wings of Desire* after Damiel as human has his first cup of coffee at a hot-dog stand: he looks up delighted about the new experience, as the camera cuts to a point-of-view shot from his perspective of a brick wall that displays a piece of graffiti, "Waiting for Godard"—a filmic in-joke paying homage to legendary filmmaker and icon of the French "New Wave," Jean-Luc Godard, as well as a high-brow reference to Samuel Beckett's famous play, *Waiting for Godot* (1953) that addresses, in an absurdist manner, existential questions concerning faith and the possibility of redemption. Perhaps the film here is expressing the hope that an experienced storyteller will appear to help wrap up the film's storyline . . .

Another aspect that endows the film with a sense of playfulness, and that goes a long way towards counterbalancing the potential portentousness of the script, is the deft use of improvisation. Given the aesthetic complexity and thematic richness of the film,

Damiel notices "Waiting for Godard" graffiti.

it is perhaps surprising to learn that much of it was based on improvisation, a method Wenders had employed in some of his earlier films. Early draft scripts suggest that there was a general idea of a two-part film, with the first part concerning a collage of observations on everyday life in the city, out of which a love story emerges in part two. Many of the vignettes of the film's first part were elaborately detailed from the outset, yet much of the remainder of the storyline surrounding Damiel falling in love with trapeze-artist Marion only emerged during the shooting, with Wenders and his team experimenting until they found a solution that felt right. There is also Peter Falk's elaborate improvisation on the American film set as he looks for a hat suitable to his private-eye character that makes him "look like a German, I wanna look anonymous." For some three minutes out of the film's total 128 minutes, Falk here plays the disgruntled film star forever dissatisfied with the props available to him, dismissing each hat as inappropriate ("this one is for the opera," "this is a bookmaker here," "they all look like gangsters' hats,"

The "film star" Peter Falk trying on hats.

"this one, I'm getting married," "this is for London, a horseshow in London"), even adopting a fake "Charlie Chan" accent, before settling for one, even though, in his words, "it ain't great."[35]

Perhaps luckily, though, not all of the improvisations on set made it into the final film. For instance, Wenders had the good sense to eliminate a scene that was to follow the encounter between Marion and Damiel in the Esplanade barroom: as she enters the room, three cream pies are briefly seen on a table in front of the bar. The presence of these cakes in a nightclub setting is left unexplained. One of the outtakes on the DVD release of the film actually shows a cream pie fight, a lighthearted slapstick sequence that was intended to undercut the pathos—or, as some would say, bathos—of the preceding scene. Cassiel, after himself having become human, was supposed to show up at the bar and challenge Damiel to a cream pie fight. Here, the childlike playfulness that pervades much of the film would have run the risk of turning into awkward childishness. It is hard to imagine what critics and audiences would have made of the scene with its awkward attempt at heavy-handed humor had it been left in the film.

Anglo-American Pop Culture: "Saved by Rock 'n' Roll"

Perhaps the most famous, and most frequently quoted, dialog line to occur in a Wenders film is Bruno Winter's comment in *Kings of the Road* bemoaning the impact of US-American cultural influence on Germans, "the Yanks have colonized our sub-conscious." Wenders may complain about this "colonization," yet it is clear that this ostensible taking-over of a national and individual psyche was and is far from unilateral and unwelcome. Wenders himself has acknowledged the potentially liberating effect that Anglo-American and African-American popular culture has had on his development as a person and as an artist. In a speech entitled "Talking about Germany," delivered in Munich in November 1991, Wenders recounted the emotionally repressive climate as he grew up in the 1950s in a West Germany reluctant to address its problematic past. In this context, Wenders states, he experienced American popular culture as fonts of visceral pleasure, leading him to indulge "so fervently in the imported pleasures that were available: American comics, American films, and American music."[36] Wenders is fond of quoting a line from a Velvet Underground song penned by Lou Reed in the late 1960s, that his "Life was saved by rock 'n' roll."

It is then perhaps no surprise that his early efforts at film display an indebtedness to aspects of American popular culture. In many ways, for instance, some of Wenders's early films emulate American gangster films, and they are set to music by popular American and British rock artists of the period, to the point that they amount to music videos *avant la lettre*. Wenders had started out with a series of short films that chronicle his preoccupation with icons of American pop culture, such as pinball machines (*Same Player Shoots Again*,

1967) and American music (*Silver City Revisited*, 1968, and *Alabama: 2000 Light Years*, 1969). He went on to direct his graduation film, *Summer in the City* (1970)—as noted before, the film's English title was taken from the 1966 hit single by the Lovin' Spoonful—that bears the subtitle, "dedicated to the [British rock band] Kinks." It includes music from both bands, as well as Gene Vincent and Chuck Berry. Even some of his later films, notably *Till the End of the World* (1991) and *The Million Dollar Hotel* (2000), feature moments that evoke the aesthetic of music videos, when the storyline is put on hold and a musical performance, either on screen or off, takes over.

Wenders shares this preoccupation with Anglo-American popular music with Handke, whose own first solo effort as a director for television, *Die Chronik der laufenden Ereignisse* (*The Chronicle of Current Events*, 1971), is replete with shots of Americana. Handke later devoted an entire book to the jukebox as the machine that distributed Anglo-American pop music across the world, *Versuch über die Jukebox* (*Essay on the Jukebox*, published 1990). Several of Handke's novels revolve around male protagonists making sojourns in the United States.

Despite being set in West Berlin, which prided itself on its thriving alternative music scene (including bands, such as Ideal and Die Ärzte, singing in German, in the wake of the *Neue Deutsche Welle* boom of the early 1980s), and was home to important singer-songwriters such as Reinhard Mey, Klaus Hoffmann, and Rio Reiser, as well as world-class ensembles such as the Berlin Philharmonic Orchestra and the Deutsche Oper, *Wings of Desire* features virtually no music that is identifiably German. The atmospheric, extra-diegetic soundtrack, composed by Jürgen Knieper, offers a collage of indistinct voices, which we associate with the "inner voices" of the inhabitants of the city, out of which emerge ethereal chords that accompany a melancholy cello. The "circus music," featuring accordion and saxophone, was provided by French composer Laurent Petitgand, who appears in the film as a circus musician. The film's soundtrack also features brief excerpts of a track by German industrial combo Sprung aus den Wolken: first, when a distraught young man, in James Dean pose, is shown sitting on his bed in an apartment; then, when Marion sits in the spot abandoned by the circus—yet the song's French title, "Pas attendre" (Don't wait) clearly disassociates the track from anything identifiably German.[37] Post-punk German band Die Haut is also credited for their jangly instrumental, "Der Karibische Western." Other brief contributions, by Israeli indie rockers Minimal Compact ("When I Go") and by American performance artist Laurie Anderson ("Angel Fragments," inspired by Walter Benjamin), likewise have little overt connection to a German musical tradition.

The film's diegetic world is dominated by the global vernacular of Anglo-American popular music, encapsulated in two cameo appearances by well-known Australian expatriate artists, both based at the time in West Berlin. The first such cameo in the Esplanade night club features the industrial rock band Crime and the City Solution, whose performance is slightly marred by the awkward attempts by undulating lead singer Simon Bonney at lip synching to the jarringly syncopated soundtrack of the song "Six Bells Chime." The second cameo appearance, at the same venue, features singer Nick Cave and his multinational band The Bad Seeds, offering broody gothic drones to a crowd of hipsters with their ultra-cool late 1980s haircuts and appropriately disenchanted black outfits. The presence of people from various countries in the performance venue (musicians from Australia, Britain, and Germany and audience members from France and as far away as Japan) hints at the existence of a globalized pop culture based on Anglo-American models that largely erases specific local traditions. No effort is made at critiquing this homogenization of culture across the globe, it is merely acknowledged as given, perhaps even celebrated.

Likewise, while the inane film project that the American crew is undertaking in an abandoned Second World War bunker may be

Crime and the City Solution, performing in the Esplanade club.

Nick Cave and The Bad Seeds, performing in the Esplanade club.

subjected to an implicit critique, the presence of Peter Falk as the "film star" is shown as welcome and refreshing. Falk engages in skeptical banter with a young German boy, who tries to convince him that a "double" took over after Hitler's suicide. Dismissing such conjecture as implausible, Falk all the same admits that the plot of the film he is working on is equally "dopey."[38] Neither the Germans nor the Americans, Wenders seems to say here, are capable of representing German history with the appropriate respect for authenticity and historical truthfulness. Both are engaged in willful historical mystification.

The fact that the US-American film-within-the-film project touches on German history in general, and on the Holocaust in particular, evokes a controversy that raged in West Germany in the early 1980s. Following the spectacular success of the American-made TV mini-series *Holocaust* (directed by Marvin J. Chomsky, 1978) in 1979, West German intellectuals and artists had expressed misgivings about what they considered the undue "appropriation" of German history by Americans. West German film maker Edgar Reitz in particular objected to the reduction of a vast, complicated, and multifaceted historical catastrophe into the manageable pop-cultural form of a melodrama revolving around a single family. Much to the critics' chagrin, however, it was precisely the emotional appeal of the focus on the story of a limited number of individuals that West German TV audiences found cathartic, resulting in an unprecedented outpouring of positive viewer feedback. The controversy surrounding the *Holocaust* mini-series prompted Reitz, who had been one of the original instigators of the "Young German Film" of the early 1960s, to embark on his vast project of narrating the German experience of the twentieth century from a German perspective in his *Heimat* project: based on notes taken in 1979, Reitz initially produced a documentary about everyday life in the Hunsrück province where he was born, before scripting and directing a series of eleven episodes that took over three years to film and that was aired on West German television, to great acclaim, in the fall of 1984. Episodes in this first series of *Heimat*, subtitled, "A German Chronicle," alternate between black-and-white and color film stock to highlight emotionally charged moments or reminiscences in a manner that anticipates Wenders's use of the device.

Wenders's *Wings of Desire*, it can be said, takes up concerns similar to those of Reitz regarding the "Hollywoodization" of German history, though in a more overtly symbolic and allegorical register, by concentrating on a few days in a specific, historically charged location, Cold War West Berlin. At one point, a TV screen is shown with Peter Falk being interviewed on the set of the American film project, where he gives an outline of its storyline: "Story: 1945, Berlin, war: I'm an American detective, a German-American guy hires me, his brother's son is in Germany . . . go to Germany, find them, the brother is dead, the family is lost, I find the kid."[39] The interviewer's response, a skeptical off-screen "In 1945?," makes it clear that the American film-within-the-film is based on absurd premises. Not only does it not heed basic notions of plausibility concerning detective work in the chaos of wartime, but it also operates with visual and thematic clichés that blithely disregard historical accuracy: the air raid shelter in the bunker in the film is populated with extras wearing the Star of David, that is, people identified as Jewish. In 1945, the only Jewish people left in Berlin would have been in hiding and would not have worn the marker on their clothing, and nobody wearing a Star of David would have been allowed into air raid shelters. It would seem then that a product of popular fiction for a mass market, such as the American film project, requires easily recognizable markers—swastika flags, Stars of David—simply because they immediately evoke Nazi Germany, regardless of historical accuracy. By highlighting such absurd incongruities, Wenders aims to wrest the telling of German stories from the Hollywood industry by offering uniquely German perspectives, thereby seeking to correct the inevitable distortions and misrepresentations that occur in American popular media.

Nazis, Jews, and a pinball machine, on the film set in the bunker.

Love and Surrender: "From Her to Eternity"

The film's conceit of a (male) angel falling in love with a (female) circus performer, to be sure, creates a strange asymmetry in that it inherently seems to privilege the male perspective: it is Damiel who has unfettered access to Marion's physical and mental world; it is he who can "appear" in her dreams; it is he who can enter her intimate space and observe her without her being aware. To a certain extent, the camera fetishizes Marion's beautiful body, as she appears as a scantily clad trapeze artist and nearly naked in her caravan trailer. Damiel's, and the camera's, initially empathetic gaze clearly becomes eroticized in the encounters with Marion, potentially creating discomfort primarily with female audiences. Yet erotic desire is visually linked with genuine human concern for the well-being of the other person: the camera turns to color—which we learn is associated with human emotions—for the first time when Marion threatens to fall from the trapeze, as Damiel watches, perhaps indicating that he is

Marion practicing her trapeze act.

worried about her injuring herself. The film takes great pains to avoid, or at least reduce, an objectification of women—the "inner monologues" of the various people we overhear are devoid of sexual content, their musings are sanitized of any prurience and elevated to a poetic, existential level.

Time and again, the film visually tries to counteract the potential asymmetry between these two protagonists by endowing Marion with angelic attributes, too: when we first see her practicing in the circus, Marion's costume features feathered wings that visually render her an "angel" of sorts, thus suggesting a kinship with Damiel from the beginning. The dialog in this scene also counteracts the pathos inherent in the angel/human dynamic by way of including humor, for instance when Marion complains that her winged costume makes her look like a "Suppenhuhn" (soup chicken), or when one of the circus workers comments, as she walks past him, "Look, an angel is walking by," briefly provoking Damiel's concern that this remark may refer to him and that he might have been discovered.[40]

The blending of actor and character also serves to mitigate some of the potential asymmetry of the relationship: Damiel displays genuine interest in Marion's personal story, as he peruses the pictures and mementos from Solveig Dommartin's past that decorate Marion's trailer. In the French release version of the film, *Les ailes du désir*, Marion's voiceover musings as well as the dialogs are in French, and even in the German original, parts of her inner monologs are in French, most notably the moment when she expresses her desire to love: in the German film Marion speaks of her "envi d'aimer," yet the published script translates this into German, "Lust zu lieben."[41] Much of Marion's musing is taken from the diaries of Peter Handke, published in 1977 under the title *Das Gewicht der Welt* (*The Weight of the World*). Wim Wenders had given a French translation of the book, entitled *Le Poids du Monde*, to Solveig Dommartin, his then partner, as a present to read. Dommartin underlined passages she found particularly meaningful, and it is these passages that are spoken, in their original German, in Marion's inner monologues, in a sense turning the male author's words into expressions of her character's female subjectivity. Yet the fact that it was Dommartin who selected the passages makes her into a kind of co-author of these texts. Moreover, at one point Marion's voice takes over from Damiel, as she quotes Handke's poem, "When the Child Was a Child." It is the passage about identity, "Warum bin ich Ich, und warum nicht Du?" (Why am I I, and not You?), establishing a congruence of male author and female speaker. As Damiel appears in her dream, Marion varies the poem by inserting a line, mumbling in her sleep, "I want you to stay with me" (in French, Dommartin's native language, although the printed script again gives the phrase in German, "Ich will, daß du bei mir bleibst").[42] A close-up shows her hand meeting that of Damiel, suggesting a reciprocity in the choice of partner.

On one level, the film revolves around male desire to be united with a female, with the angel-meets-trapeze-artist a poetically heightened (some would say, inflated) version of a conventional

Damiel appears to Marion in her dream.

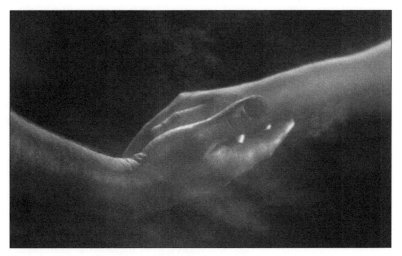

Marion's and Damiel's hands join in her dream.

boy-meets-girl story. To what extent can it be argued that a woman, Marion, is here turned into a kind of mouthpiece for male concerns, ventriloquizing male preoccupations and desires? After all, she voices her desire for Damiel when he has managed to invade her dream, thus perhaps manipulating her to respond to *his* desire. Perhaps this is the ultimate male fantasy—male authors inventing a female character whose desires "spontaneously" align with those of the male protagonist? Perhaps we are dealing here, as I put it in an earlier article on the film, with a "projection of male desire onto the female, since it is implied that the woman here desires precisely what the man wants her (or makes her want) to desire."[43] Yet the fact that some of Marion's lines are in French, as well as some visual clues, such as the personal memorabilia associated with Dommartin the actress, suggest that Wenders at least tries to counterbalance the tendency of the plot-line to privilege a male perspective and is making gestures toward acknowledging female subjecthood. It is up to each viewer to determine whether such gestures actually succeed in mitigating the film's inherent male bias.

Perhaps the most problematic part of the film is the final encounter between Damiel and Marion in the Esplanade rock club. In her chic red dress (designed by legendary Japanese fashion designer Yohji Yamamoto), Marion is clearly eroticized as she enters the barroom. Subtly, however, gender hierarchies begin to be inverted: Marion wears earrings in the shape of angel wings, symbolically rendering her into an angel, whereas Damiel has forfeited his stature as an angel and become an ordinary human. With somnambulistic assurance, Marion walks toward Damiel, whom she quite literally recognizes as the "man of her dreams," and begins a lengthy monolog (weighed down by Peter Handke's potentially portentous rhetoric) that takes up nearly six minutes towards the end of the film's 128 minutes. In Handke's draft manuscript, the monolog is prefaced by the phrase "Die Frau hat das Wort" ("Woman takes the floor," literally, "Woman has the word")—an ambivalent formulation that can connote both that it is the woman who actively seizes the opportunity to speak and that it is a gesture of the male author ceding the floor to the female.[44]

The scene has been subjected to substantial criticism, not least for its language, described, for instance, by Wolfram Schütte of the *Frankfurter Rundschau*, as "contrived bombast" (verstiegenen Schwulst).[45] Similar charges had been leveled against the soliloquies by Nova, the symbolic female protagonist of Handke's drama, *Über die Dörfer*, which Wim Wenders directed at the Salzburg Festival in 1982. Likewise, Marion embarks on protracted quasi-metaphysical musings as *Wings of Desire* drops any pretense at filmic realism and altogether shifts into a symbolic register. Phrases such as "we are sitting in the people's square" (Wir sitzen auf dem Platz des Volkes), a square full of people "who all desire the same thing as we do" (alle wünschen sich dasselbe wie wir), and the claim that Marion and Damiel will inaugurate a "history of giants" (Geschichte von Riesen) or become "new ancestors" (Stammeltern) raise the question whether Handke truly succeeded in cleansing the German language of the tainted linguistic legacy of the Third Reich. Terms such as "Volk," with its suggestion of unquestioned congruence of individual wills, "Riesen," with its potential association with the notion of the Nietzschean *Übermensch*, as well as "Stammeltern," evoking uneasy thoughts of racial eugenics and the breeding of an Aryan "master race," all have an altogether ominous ring to German ears.

Yet, again, it can be argued that the visual construction of the scene seeks to minimize its politically potentially problematic overtones, initially by endowing the encounter between Damiel-as-man and Marion the woman with quasi-religious significance: Damiel hands Marion a chalice with wine, from which she drinks, turning the scene into a kind of religious communion. She gently pushes him back as he leans forward with his chest toward her, before she begins her extended soliloquy. After a while, the camera moves from a medium close-up showing the two characters facing each other to a sequence of extreme close-ups: Marion looks directly into the camera, thus

Marion's encounter with Damiel: the chalice.

addressing her declaration of love not only to Damiel (whose point of view the camera adopts here) but also to the audience. Her soliloquy, in which she claims to be speaking for all of humankind, thus becomes a kind of manifesto of inclusion, compassion, and hopefulness. Likewise, Damiel's silent response culminates in an extreme close-up of his smiling face, directed, again, both at Marion and at the audience at large. Their "loving gazes" are aimed at us, the viewers, too. Marion's declaration of love is thus addressed to the audience, becoming a gesture of inclusion and a gesture that seeks to engender community.

Like Marion's soliloquy, Damiel's musings that follow the lovers' first night together are embedded in a larger audiovisual and structural context that affects the manner in which we (are supposed to) read these scenes: Damiel is shown supporting Marion as she practices her act on the vertical rope: visually, differential hierarchies that may have obtained earlier between male and female here have been reversed, as the male is here shown to be subservient to female

Marion's declaration of love, directed at Damiel / the camera / us.

Damiel's reaction, directed at Marion / the camera / us.

self-fulfillment. A cynical viewer could argue that, much like the love-struck Professor Rath in Josef von Sternberg's *The Blue Angel* (1930), who lost his high social position and became a hapless clown when he fell in love with cabaret artist Lola Lola (Marlene Dietrich), Damiel has been reduced to the status of an auxiliary to a circus performer. Peter Falk had earlier invoked the name of Emil Jannings, the actor who played Professor Rath in von Sternberg's film. Wenders's film inverts the "fallen angel" motif, elevating the figure of Marion to near God-like status. Earlier on, as a trapeze artist, Marion was radically separated from Damiel the angel, who uneasily paced about the circus ring, nervously watching her perform above. Now, by way of contrast, the vertical rope creates a kind of umbilical cord between two humans, suggesting a reciprocity between performer and supporter: two separate individuals have bonded to become a couple, jointly forming a new entity. Moreover, the film here becomes overtly self-referential: the "immortal image" that Damiel hails as having emerged from his encounter with Marion, it can be said, is the film we are watching and whose images will resonate in our minds.

The two scenes with Damiel and Marion display a strained indebtedness to key concerns of German Romanticism: the whimsical playfulness of the earlier parts of the film, reminiscent of E. T. A. Hoffmann's flights of poetic imagination, where anything was possible, are here replaced by the questionable metaphysics of love espoused by authors such as Friedrich Schlegel and Novalis. Moreover, the heavy religious overtones of the scenes hark back to Novalis's nostalgic idealization of pre-Reformation Christianity as a source of spiritual redemption and societal harmony. The shift toward fairy tale is complete, as practical questions concerning the relationship between Damiel and Marion—Where did they spend the night? How did they gain access to the Esplanade club after hours? Why are they practicing a vertical rope act together?—are superseded by overtly symbolic concerns.

The film's key concept of "homecoming" can itself be viewed as derived from German Romanticism, with Damiel as the archetypal lone wanderer who has come to rest. His voiceover emphasizes the notion of togetherness, expressed in highly symbolic language, stating that he experiences his encounter with Marion as a kind of rebirth or "homecoming," as a conjoining of disparate parts into a person:

> Only amazement
> about the two of us,
> amazement about Man and Woman
> has made a Human out of me.[46]

Damiel equates his falling in love with an ascent into true personhood, his journey ending on an optimistic note. Yet the union between man and woman, it seems, comes at a price: as Marion practices on the vertical rope with Damiel's help, Cassiel is shown sitting on the floor, looking on, visually excluded and isolated within a black-and-white cameo inside the images in color. From today's perspective, the paean to the love between "Man and Woman" that turned Damiel fully into a human being may appear uncomfortably heteronormative, seemingly excluding same-sex relationships. Could it be that the celebration of (heterosexual) love is at the expense of male friendship? The (homosocial) bonding Damiel used to enjoy with Cassiel? Damiel's transformation into a human may have led him, "from eternity to her"—reversing the words of the Nick Cave song[47]—that preceded the encounter with Marion—, but it also separated him from Cassiel, from what used to be his most significant interpersonal (if that word can be used for angels) relationship . . .

The Weight of History: Labor of Mourning

Among the most remarkable images in *Wings of Desire* are those depicting the interior of the Staatsbibliothek near Potsdamer Platz.

Cassiel (in black-and-white) looks on as Marion and Damiel practice.

The repository of human knowledge and sanctuary of remembrance in the form of books is also the place of residence of the angels, as collectors and guardians of historical memory. Early on, as the angels wander through West Berlin's State Library, a female voice is heard, reading:

> In 1921, Walter Benjamin purchased Paul Klee's watercolor *Angelus Novus* ... In his final writing, *On the Concept of History* (1940), he interpreted the image as an allegory of a retrospective view on history.[48]

This key quotation highlights the film's indebtedness to Walter Benjamin's philosophy of history. It is unfortunate that the reference may be lost on English-speaking viewers, since it is not translated in the subtitles of the English version.

Paul Klee's famous watercolor shows a delicate figure with angel wings and a wide-eyed face with open mouth, looking directly at the viewer, as if in shock. The reference to Benjamin, the German-

Jewish cultural critic and philosopher, and his concept of the "Angel of History" as outlined in his ninth thesis on the concept of history, clearly aligns *Wings of Desire* with Benjamin's notion of history as perpetual catastrophe and Wenders's angels with Benjamin's transcendental witness of this catastrophe. The film enacts this view by way of repeatedly splicing documentary footage of the wartime destruction of Berlin into the present story. This footage, as Xavier Vila and Alice Kuzniar have pointed out, "resists integration into narrative."[49] Moreover, Cassiel's desperate leap from the top of the Siegessäule following the suicide of a young man, with its rapid succession of shots from an unstable, handheld camera that show brief glimpses of urban despair—a drug addict collapsing at a telephone booth, a frightened child crying—alternating with documentary footage of wartime aerial bombings, is a clear visualization of Benjamin's pessimistic assessment of human history as perpetual catastrophe. Just as Paul Klee's angel, in Benjamin's interpretation, recoils from the onslaught of distressing historical events, Wenders's Cassiel—whose name was identified by one of the readers in the library as that of "the angel of solitude and tears"[50]—seems to despair that he can only witness human suffering but not prevent or mend disaster. A link is made between historical wartime trauma and an alienated, violent present that characterizes the city, and the angels are presented as empathetic but largely ineffectual onlookers.

The unnamed character identified as "Homer" in the published script is perhaps the most poignant reminder of the weight of German history as it bears upon the city. The character is played by Curt Bois, whose biography encapsulates much of German history of the twentieth century, as well as German film history. Born in 1901 in Berlin to Jewish parents, Bois was one of the first child stars of early German cinema, appearing as early as 1908 as "Heinerle" in a series of short sound-film vignettes and gramophone recordings from Leo Fall's popular operetta, *Der fidele Bauer* (*The Merry Peasant*). Young Curt then headed his own series of short film comedies, usually playing a street-smart, wise-cracking boy who plays pranks upon grown-ups. As an adult, too, Bois was one of the few actors on the German silent screen who excelled in physical comedy. For instance, in Ernst Lubitsch's *Die Austernprinzessin* (*The Oyster Princess*, 1919) he is featured as the crazed bandleader who with grotesque contortions conducts an on-screen orchestra during the frenzied "foxtrot epidemic" dance sequence. *Wings of Desire* pays homage to this tradition of physical comedy when the exhausted Homer sits down on an armchair on a landing of the staircase inside the library and tries to put on his eyeglasses, which initially refuse to cooperate—the bit of whimsical fidgeting was improvised by Bois on the spot.

During the Weimar era, Bois appeared in numerous comedy films, most notably as an uptight fashion salesman in Richard Eichberg's *Der Fürst von Pappenheim* (*The Prince of Pappenheim*, 1927). The famous cross-dressing sequence, in which Bois dons female attire stepping in for a model who failed to show up for a fashion show, was used in the notorious anti-Semitic propaganda film *Der ewige Jude* (*The Eternal Jew*, dir. Fritz Hippler, 1940) as so-called "evidence" of supposed Jewish decadence and depravity. During the 1920s and early 1930s, with his understated, razor-sharp wit and crisp diction, Bois also had a successful career as an actor on the stage and as a recording artist. After the Nazis came to power, he emigrated to Hollywood, where he appeared as a bit player in countless films, including a noted cameo as a sleazy pickpocket in Michael Curtiz's *Casablanca* (1942). Returning to Germany in the early 1950s, Bois performed at Bertolt Brecht's theater in East Berlin, portraying the sly landowner Puntila in *Herr Puntila und sein Knecht Matti* (*Mr. Puntila and His Manservant Matti*), a role he reprised in the film version directed by Alberto Cavalcanti, released in 1960. His remarkable career was rounded off by innumerable appearances on the West German popular stage, in often mediocre genre films, and on television. His participation in *Wings of Desire* was his final appearance as an actor in a full-length feature film. Although some scenes were shot that showed Otto Sanders and Curt Bois after the fall of the Wall, Bois died before the filming of *Faraway, So Close!*, the sequel to *Wings of Desire* that chronicles the story of Cassiel.

In Wenders's film, then, the allegorical character played by Bois stands for the long history of German cinema and twentieth-century popular culture, with their various historical ruptures; for the glamor of Weimar-era entertainment culture that was all but destroyed by the Nazis; for the fate of racially persecuted emigrants during exile and after their return; and for the disappearance of a cosmopolitan German popular culture (which had largely been the product of artists and entertainers of Jewish descent). Homer's on-screen musings on the necessity of a common narrative (the "Epic of Peace") as the basis for social cohesion not only address issues of high culture but also extol the role that popular culture plays in facilitating such cohesion. It is particularly poignant that it is the once famous and revered entertainer, the traumatized, formerly exiled Jew, who mourns the absence of cultural unity and reflects upon the presence of history, as he wanders across the desolate wasteland of 1980s Potsdamer Platz, searching in vain for the busy center of the bustling metropolis he once inhabited and the Café Josty he used to frequent. To be sure, when Homer notes that all of a sudden "banners appeared all over the place" and "people were no longer friendly, nor was the police," such references to the emergence of National Socialism, to persecution, expulsion, and exile remain rather abstract and vague, to the point of glossing over the extreme violence that accompanied the collapse of Weimar Germany as a pluralistic, liberal democracy.

Despite its serious content, the sequence showing Homer, accompanied by a concerned Cassiel, expressing his distress that the Potsdamer Platz he used to know as a young man is nowhere to be found, has its own peculiar whimsy: as Homer and Cassiel wander around the no-man's-land near the Wall, we see two men in the top right corner of the frame walking on a strange contraption. It is the track of the Magnetbahn, an experimental elevated transportation system that had been put into testing there in 1984 and was, at the time of filming *Wings of Desire*, not yet operational.[51] It is not clear whether the shots of two pairs of men walking in the same frame was intentional—it very much looks as if some strangers just happened to pass by during the filming of the scene. The situation is even more puzzling, when Homer, exhausted, sits down on an armchair abandoned in the middle of the wasteland and we can again see someone walking on the elevated magnet railway track far in the background—here, too, it is unclear whether this juxtaposition was intentional or may be of symbolic significance. The presence of these passers-by is not commented upon, but it creates a strange, whimsical and potentially distracting, visual parallelism between the main story unfolding in the foreground and the, perhaps coincidental, goings-on in the background at moments of extremely charged thematic significance. A similar tension emerges later on, during Damiel and Cassiel's walk inside the "Death Strip," when the presence of numerous rabbits in the background potentially distracts from the angels' conversation concerning Damiel's resolve to become human. It turns out that this, too, is an oddly realistic detail: because rabbits were light enough not to trigger the landmines planted inside the "Death Strip," the area became a safe habitat where the animals could breed without the interference of predators. Wenders acknowledged this bizarre ironic tidbit of the city's tragic division by deliberately including rabbits in the sequence, filmed in an artificially constructed replica of the "Death Strip"—since filming in the actual space was impossible.

One of the ironies concerning Wenders's ambivalent fascination with Anglo-American popular culture is that what after the Second World War counted as acceptable, historically untainted German popular culture of the Weimar era had itself arisen out of a reflexive interaction with Anglo-American and African-American impulses.

Homer and Cassiel, on Potsdamer Platz, with two men on the Magnetbahn.

This culture survived precariously abroad in exile and had to be re-imported, so to speak, from countries such as Great Britain and the United States after the collapse of National Socialism. The German-Jewish tradition represented by Curt Bois, then, is to a certain extent something brought in from "outside" as much as were Hollywood movies, jazz, rock 'n' roll, and other forms of Anglo-American/African-American popular music. Culture, it seems, whether high-brow or popular, is always already inherently hybrid, putting the lie on notions of purity and indigeneity. *Wings of Desire* acknowledges and celebrates such mixing.

With his quest to identify historical sites and to forge a story that binds people together, Homer attempts to perform the labor of mourning that enables a society to move on. Like the angels, he resides in the library, the sanctuary of memory. We see Homer contemplate history in cosmological terms while sitting among terrestrial globes, and for him, a coffee-table book of portrait photographs "comes alive": under his gaze, the photos of August Sander's Weimar-era

Menschen des 20. Jahrhunderts (*Twentieth-Century Humans*, 1929) morph into documentary footage of Berlin streets during and after bombing raids in the Second World War.

It seems highly significant that the character of Homer remains by himself—we hear his musings but never see him interact with other people—and that he seems to be able, like the children, to sense the presence of the angels. The traumatized rémigré remains isolated, not integrated into mainstream culture, but to a certain extent privileged as well—he may very well, like the Peter Falk character, be a former angel himself. Homer is the one who bears witness to the catastrophes that continue to exert their impact on present-day Berlin, as a kind of modern-day shaman, performing an essential task on behalf of an entire community.

This task involves the creating of narratives. In ancient Greece, it was Homer who provided the foundation of a culture by way of constructing epic stories, *The Iliad* and *The Odyssey*, that gave the members of a community a sense of collective identity. Echoing ideas expressed by Walter Benjamin in his seminal essay, "Der Erzähler" ("The Narrator. Reflections on the Works of Nikolai Leskow," 1933), the Homer of Wenders and Handke laments the disappearance of unifying narratives and the erosion of an organic relationship between storyteller and audience. In modernity, the community of listeners sitting around a storyteller in a shared space has been replaced by readers isolated both from the storyteller and from one another. Thus, the community-building qualities of narration have disappeared. The film's Homer laments this situation and seeks to rectify it, in an effort to provide the basis for a new identity, by way of an "Epic of Peace."

Unlike the Homer figure, the (West) Berliners we encounter in Wenders's film have little interest in the historical significance of their surroundings or in traces of the past. Nor are they undertaking the kind of labor of mourning the old man muses is necessary for collective healing. Insofar as Curt Bois in a sense stands for German film in general, Wenders seems to suggest that he as a filmmaker has to perform the labor of mourning the destruction of German-Jewish culture himself, and *Wings of Desire* can be read as an attempt to do just that. Yet, to a certain extent, *Wings of Desire* exhibits a peculiar kind of potential blind spot: Homer's musings do not primarily revolve around his own fate as a refugee or that of others who were persecuted or attacked by the brutal forces of the Third Reich. Instead, the documentary war-time footage inserted into the film focuses upon moments when the war affected those who had not been persecuted, those who had stayed home. In lamenting the devastation wrought by aerial bombardments upon Berlin, the film runs the risk of blurring important historical distinctions: visually, it would seem that the Germans themselves could be viewed as the primary victims of the war, especially since much of the footage focuses on civilian suffering, including images of dead children.

Loose Ends and Open Endings: Widening the Circle

I think it is fair to say that Wenders has always had problems with narrative, an issue he himself has repeatedly acknowledged.[52] He started out as a painter, and his strength as a filmmaker primarily lies in his power of observation and visual construction. His films abound in compelling images, visually stunning arrangements that project a sense of authentic insight and profound truth. *Wings of Desire* abounds with such visually and thematically rich images and sequences. In addition to many of the seemingly random vignettes of everyday city life, the scene with the dying motorcyclist stands out, as does the mirror scene in Marion's trailer. Together with Henri Alekan's sublime camera work, Wenders here creates filmic moments that somehow "ring true."

In historical or political terms, perhaps the most significant such moment is the scene with Damiel and Cassiel on the "Death Strip" on the eastern side of the Wall that leads into Damiel's crossing-over into human existence. Here, as the black-and-white footage turns to color, Damiel holds a stone to his forehead, contemplating what it might mean to have weight, to have a body. Cut to a point-of-view shot of Cassiel, in black-and-white, who notices that Damiel has begun to leave footprints in the soil, soil meticulously raked to show traces of anybody who may have entered the forbidden zone and attempted to escape to the West. The camera slowly pans sideways to reveal that the East German border guards have not noticed anything suspicious. Cassiel looks around, his face displaying grave concern. This is perhaps the film's most heart-stopping moment: anybody attempting to walk along this "Death Strip" would trigger the land mines buried underneath the soil, running the risk of being blown to pieces. The message is clear: in forfeiting his privileged existence as an angel and becoming human, Damiel exposes himself to the risk of horrific bodily injury and an equally horrific death. Sensing this, Cassiel quickly picks Damiel up and "carries" him across to the western side of the Wall, out of harm's way. With a few filmic strokes, Wenders has made a profound point about mortality as the basic existential truth of the human condition: to be alive means to be vulnerable to injury and to have to die one day.

Damiel's story after becoming human is wrapped up at considerable speed. The logic of the main poetic conceit unfolds with charming consistency: when Damiel wakes up in front of the western side of the Wall, his armor drops on him with a loud noise, leaving him with an injury on his head. (An interspersed shot from Damiel's now human point of view showing a helicopter hovering above creates a humorous ambiguity as to the origin of the armor.) Thus, Damiel's first experience as a human is an injury. With great curiosity and interest he notes the slight pain, touches his head and looks at the bright red of the blood on his fingers, before licking them to experience what it tastes like. Damiel may not have acquired a childhood in the customary sense of a biography, but he displays

Damiel's first human experience: licking his blood after an injury.

the kind of "childship" articulated in the film's leitmotif poem. As he sets out to explore the city on foot, he takes in his new experiences with a sense of wonder and bemusement. Gentle humor persists as we viewers watch his childlike awkwardness and his lack of social graces: he asks a passer-by to name and explain colors to him, sells his armor at an antique shop and buys himself a freakishly tasteless outfit (as well as a watch) with the money. He seeks out Peter Falk at the film set to let his American "compañero" know that he has become human, only to find out that Falk himself used to be an angel. Damiel's inquisitive curiosity is rebuffed by Falk, who tells him that he has to find things out for himself—"That's the fun of it!"[53] Damiel experiences the frustration of having lost his angelic mobility and omniscience as he wanders around town in search of Marion. He learns about the mundane inconveniences of being human, feeling a slight stomach pain after having relished his first cup of black coffee (presumably, upon an empty stomach). As he sits in the middle of the abandoned circus ring contemplating what to do next, he responds to the inquiries of two boys on what the matter is with him with disarming directness: "Mangel" ("Need," literally, "Lack"), a statement concerning the absence of Marion that is, of course, incomprehensible to the boys. Remnants of his angelic omniscience re-emerge as he ties a loose shoelace for one of the boys, stating, with bossy assurance, "a double knot is the only way to make it hold."[54]

The humor surrounding Damiel is complemented by that surrounding Marion: standing by a hot-dog stand, she chances upon Peter Falk, who stops by for a cup of coffee. A dialog ensues in which she playfully tries to enlist his detective persona, asking him for help in locating the man—Damiel—she seeks to meet. Falk plays along while noting that, given that she knows neither the man's name nor whereabouts, this will be a "tough case." Falk then proceeds to try to recruit Cassiel, who has been watching the exchange, with the same routine that he had used on Damiel at a different hot-dog stand, "I can't see you, but I know you're there," reaching out his hand, "I'm your friend! Compañero!"[55] Our pleasure in watching these scenes comes from recognizing the motifs, phrases, and images that we had encountered already in a different context. Here and there, the rush to wrap up the story quickly may have resulted in little continuity mistakes: for instance, when Marion sits in the middle of the abandoned circus ring, her belongings are in three pieces of luggage, two suitcases and a shoulder bag. As she wanders around the city streets at night looking for the "man of her dreams," she only has the shoulder bag. In her encounter with Falk at the hot-dog stand, she has no luggage at all, yet the shoulder bag reappears a few moments later as she continues her search. Such concerns with filmic realism, however, many be largely moot, since in shifting from black-and-white to color film stock, *Wings of Desire* has long turned from filmic poem about urban alienation into cinematic fairy tale.

As already noted, early drafts of the script indicate that *Wings of Desire* was originally intended to tell the story of both angels, with

Damiel's transformation into human as a positive, Cassiel's, however, as a negative, experience. In his audio commentaries to the German and American DVD releases of the film, Wenders's wryly notes that he and his crew spent so much time and energy on filming the many black-and-white vignettes for the first part of the film that they ran out of time when it came to the transition to color after Damiel's transformation. Instead of forming the second half of the film, Damiel's story as human covers little more than half an hour out of a total of just over two hours. Cassiel's story was relegated to the sequel, *Faraway, So Close!*, which also picks up the story of Damiel and Marion some five or six years later.

Even as a separate work, *Faraway, So Close!* is an oddly sprawling film bursting at the seams with symbolically charged storylines and images. It is as if Wenders wanted to make up for potential omissions and for neglecting East Berlin in the earlier film by way of exploring the now accessible eastern parts of the city in as many locations possible. This time around, the angels do reside on top of the Brandenburg Gate, and we get a female angel as a major character, notably Nastassja Kinski as Raphaela. Not only Damiel, Cassiel, and Marion are back, but so is Peter Falk, with Willem Dafoe, as well as Mikhail Gorbachev, Lou Reed, and a host of others thrown in for good measure.

In a sense it is a good thing that *Wings of Desire* did not have to carry the additional burden of telling us what happened to Cassiel, the second angel. All the same, it is interesting to speculate what the film would have looked like had some of the original ideas survived. I already mentioned the politically charged subplot of the die-hard Nazi *Werwölfe* that were to haunt the city. The angels were originally supposed to reside not in the Staatsbibliothek near Potsdamer Platz but in one of the abandoned ruins of a former embassy in the city's Tiergarten district, the lack of a roof there perhaps giving additional significance to the German title of the film, concerning "the sky over Berlin ..." What would the film have looked like had the idea of having erstwhile West German Chancellor Willy Brandt appear as a former angel worked out, as was planned at one point? Such details would have given the film's investigation of German history a completely different spin.

Even in its present form, the film addresses more than the concerns I have touched thus far. It features a poetic sequence that starts with a succession of seemingly unrelated, beautiful shots, among them images of the light refracting on a water surface, a swarm of birds undulating in the sky, a tree trunk in the fog in the middle of a lake, reeds swaying in the wind, the crowns of trees reaching into the sky. These shots frame the second conversation between Damiel and Cassiel, occurring pretty much in the middle of the film. Here, Peter Handke's text opens up new perspectives that go beyond the manifold personal, psychological, spiritual, philosophical, historical, social, and political concerns I have explored. As the two angels walk along a canal near the Wall, their conversation shifts to what could be called a cosmic register, as they recall the first time they visited the space, in times primeval, before the advent of humans and before the city was built. Where the canal now is, Cassiel notes, there used to be the bed of a primeval river, an *Urstromtal*:

> One day, I still remember ... the glacier melted and the icebergs drifted to the north. A tree passed by, still green, with an empty bird's nest. Only the fish had leapt over a myriad of years.[56]

The images of nature, of water surfaces, birds, trees, and fish remind the viewer of the limited, anthropocentric notion we may have of history: where we think of history in terms of years, decades, and centuries, the angels have a broader outlook that encompasses millions of years, long before the appearance of humans. This puts the human history of continuous warfare, conquest, torture, enslavement, and genocide into a new perspective: we viewers may

The cosmic dimension of history.

contemplate the traumas inflicted by the catastrophic history of the twentieth century as disruption and discontinuity, but the larger cycles of destruction and renewal, of death and rebirth of nature continue regardless. This is not to negate the lamentable history of violence, as the exchange between Damiel and Cassiel makes clear. With the advent of man, Damiel notes, "began the history of wars. It is still going on," to which Cassiel replies, "But the story of the grass, the sun, the leaps and the shouts . . . is still going on, too."[57]

The realization that human history co-exists and is, ultimately, embedded in larger, natural and cosmic cycles of history, can be a source of spiritual comfort. Wenders's film admonishes us not to forget that the "Geschichte der Luftsprünge" (history of leaps into the air) continues alongside all the conflicts that mark social and political history. It is at this point that the two angels walk towards the Wall, covered with graffiti ranging from the whimsically cryptic ("Eat red apple sauce") to the culturally referential ("We can be heroes"—a line from the famous David Bowie song). And:

Cinematic miracle: Damiel and Cassiel walk through the Wall.

a cinematic "miracle" occurs as the two seem to manage to walk right through the Wall. In reminding us that nothing is permanent and that change is always possible, Wenders's cinematic fairy tale becomes a source of tremendous hope, affirming life with all its limitations and imperfections.

The Berlin depicted in the film no longer exists. The Wall that divided the city has been swept away by political change, and many of the locations at which segments of the film were shot have disappeared, replaced by new buildings. Potsdamer Platz, the empty urban wasteland near the fault line of the Cold War, is now a jumble of gleaming office towers, upscale hotels, a shopping mall, movie theaters, and a casino. High-rises now dwarf Weinhaus Huth, one of the two buildings that had survived the aerial bombings. The other, Hotel Esplanade, has been partly demolished; the rest was moved a few feet to make room for the gigantic Sony Center. The Esplanade barroom, where the two rock concerts in *Wings of Desire* take place and where Marion meets Damiel, is now encased in glass, as a bizarre kind of historic specimen preserved for the delectation of tourists. *Wings of Desire* has thus itself become a historical document, a time capsule of sorts, capturing the unique situation and ambience some two years before the Wall fell.

Damiel's story concludes with his reflecting on his experience as a human. An early draft of the script indicates that the voiceover we hear as Damiel supports Marion on her vertical rope was originally conceived as a kind of message Damiel-as-human addresses to Cassiel, who is still an angel. The final image we see of Damiel is that of his hand, writing, framed and shot in the same way as the image that opened the film. Yet the text that we see being written has changed: it is not the conclusion of the four-stanza "Song of Being a Child" that we saw emerge at the beginning of the film. In the black-and-white shot at the beginning, Damiel's writing may have expressed a wish to attain a childhood, a story of growth and unfolding, like that of all human beings. Now the shot is in color, as Damiel writes about his having become human. The sentiments expressed highlight the fact that humans are relational beings: "The amazement about the two of us, amazement about man and woman . . . has turned me into a human being." To be human means to enter into relationships with other human beings. As we listen to Damiel's voice off screen, we see his hand completing the writing of a sentence: "I now know what no angel knows."[58] On a mundane level, the sentence refers to the love story we have just witnessed, and to Damiel's sexual initiation in his relationship with Marion. On a more spiritual level, the phrase could connote that, as immaterial beings, angels have no access to corporeal knowledge. Such knowledge, the phrase seems to assert, is the unique privilege of humans. This, as Peter Falk had pointed out to Damiel earlier, "is the fun of it."

Epilogue: "To be continued"

Wings of Desire closes with a coda, showing the character of Homer in his continued quest to find Potsdamer Platz. The old man, his right hand holding up an umbrella, shuffles toward the Wall. In a shot reminiscent of the one that showed the two angels, in a different location, walking toward the Wall at the end of their conversation about the cosmic perspective on history, Homer repeats in voiceover his musings concerning society's need for a storyteller who provides a common narrative to achieve community and cohesion:

> Name the men, women and children who will look for me ... me, their storyteller, their cantor, their spokesman ... because they need me more than anything in the world.[59]

The world in general, Homer insists, is in dire need of art, to overcome alienation and to establish societal unity. These words, spoken by someone who represents the history of German film and the German-Jewish exile experience, implies that for German society to achieve cohesion, it has to embrace its own image production (German film, as opposed to Hollywood fare), and it has to seek to re-integrate the German-Jewish cultural heritage into the mainstream. Both, Wenders suggests here, are indispensable for the process of healing, for recovering from the multiple self-inflicted traumas of German twentieth-century history. In this manner, Wenders's film constitutes itself as the modern equivalent of the kind of narrative epic that the old man argues is essential for the survival of a cultural community. Watching a film in a movie theater in the presence of others, seeing a story unfold on the silver screen in a communal setting, may overcome the fragmentation and isolation that the shift from oral to written culture portended, in which the relationship between storyteller and a collective of listeners physically present in the same space was replaced by that between a distant author and isolated, distant individual readers. In imagining a new, if virtual, community, *Wings of Desire* may be said to become the "Epic of Peace" that is the object of the old man's quest.

The German-Jewish rémigré, returning to what used to be his hometown and his home country, has the final word. Or does he?

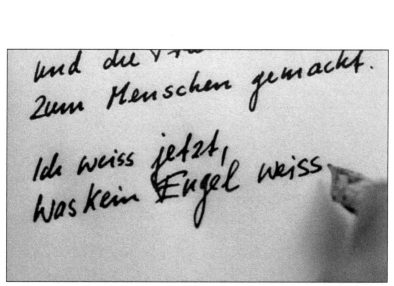

Damiel's hand writing: "I now know what no angel knows."

To be continued: storyteller Homer walks toward the Wall.

At the very end of the film, a strange doubling takes place: Homer utters the cryptic words "nous sommes embarqués" (we are embarked) as the words "Fortsetzung folgt" (To be continued) appear on the screen, over an image of a cloudy sky above the city horizon. On one level, both utterances seem to be congruent, pointing to the notion of a new beginning ("we are on our way") as well as promising a continuation ("there will be a sequel of sorts"). In the immediate context, the reference/s could be to the venture Wenders and Dommartin were involved in during the production of *Wings of Desire*, the mega-project *Till the End of the World* (released in 1991), as a film that expands the scope from present-day Berlin into the future and across the entire globe. Alternatively, the words, on a black-and-white screen, that is, shown from the perspective of the angels, could point to the need to tell the story of the second angel, Cassiel, which Wenders did in *Faraway, So Close!* (released in 1993). Yet things are more complex than that: it is of interest that Homer's words are uttered in French, the language of actress Solveig Dommartin, suggesting that the project of healing trauma and forging a new, positive sense of national identity, which may appear to be a primarily German concern, necessitates the participation and support of other nations, and that it is equally relevant for these nations as well.

A note in Handke's manuscript of the passage adds a further, somewhat puzzling dimension: the phrase "nous sommes embarqués" is followed by a reference to Blaise Pascal (1623–62).[60] In fact, the phrase turns out to be a direct quotation from a work by this French seventeenth-century mathematician and Catholic theologian, his *Pensées* (*Thoughts*), published posthumously in 1670. Here, the phrase refers to what Pascal considered an existential given: we are all placed in an existential situation ("embarked" on a kind of metaphorical boat) in which we are compelled to decide upon issues of faith, in what became known as "Pascal's Wager." It is rational, Pascal argued, to live as though God existed, since the rewards if he does are infinite (eternal life in heaven), as would be the punishment (damnation in hell), if one failed to do so. If God doesn't exist, the disadvantages of having believed in Him are minimal, by comparison. Pascal noted that we have no choice but to choose with regard to matters of faith. Faith, in Pascal's perspective, involves a kind of bet on probability, an ingenious way to combine rational thought and theological speculation.[61] Homer's final words thus add a theological layer to the ending of the film. Subliminally, Christian motifs have been present throughout, from the poem about "childship," and the Christ-like pose that Damiel strikes in the library, to the name of the trapeze artist, Marion, a form of Mary. If the angels in *Wings of Desire* were primarily metaphysical personages in the tradition of the notion of guardian angels—not to mention the transcendental addressees in Rilke's *Duino Elegies* or Benjamin's "Angel of History"—with only few Christian overtones, the sequel, *Faraway, So Close!* turns them overtly into intermediaries between humans and the Christian God.[62]

It would seem, then, that Wenders and Handke subtly seek to suggest that the solace that their filmic "Epic of Peace" promotes can perhaps only be achieved by a return to the Christian faith. In a sense, then, the ending of *Wings of Desire* would prefigure an interest on Wenders's part in an undogmatic form of Christianity, as evidenced in his recent documentary about the current Catholic pontiff, *Pope Francis: A Man of His Word* (2018). Uttered by a character from an ancient, pre-Christian tradition (Homer) in the voice of a German actor of Jewish descent (Curt Bois), the statement ostensibly advocating Christianity and the possibility of redemption is itself subject to multiple potential contradictions. The hint is so understated that few, if any, viewers are likely to pick up on the theological dimension of the film's ending. And it is unclear, if they did, whether too many viewers would be willing to "embark" on this project in those narrowly defined terms. What is clear, though, is that the quest for peace, human connection, and community has "to be continued."

CREDITS

Director:
Wim Wenders

Assistant Director:
Claire Denis

Writers:
Wim Wenders
Peter Handke
Richard Reitinger

Production Companies:
Road Movies Filmproduktion
Argos Films
Westdeutscher Rundfunk (WDR)

Produced by:
Wim Wenders (producer)
Anatole Dauman (producer)
Iris Windisch (executive producer)

Cast:
Bruno Ganz (Damiel)
Otto Sander (Cassiel)
Solveig Dommartin (Marion)
Curt Bois (Homer)
Peter Falk (himself)

Music:
Jürgen Knieper
Laurent Petitgand

Cinematography:
Henri Alekan
Agnès Godard

Film Editing:
Peter Przygodda

Art Direction:
Heidi Lühi

Costume Design:
Monika Jacobs

Runtime:
128 min.

Sound Mix:
Dolby stereo

Color:
Eastmancolor & b/w

Aspect Ratio:
1.66 : 1

Camera:
Arriflex 35 BL4

Film Length:
3,493 m

Negative Format:
35 mm

Cinematographic Process:
Spherical

Printed Film Format:
35 mm; Digital (Digital Cinema Package DCP)

Production Costs:
DM 5 Million (inflation adjusted ca. $7–9 Million in 2018)

Release Dates:
September 1987 (France), October 1987 (West Germany), April 1988 (USA)

NOTES

1   Andrew Horn, "Wim Wenders' *Wings of Desire* Soars to Screens after Restoration,"
    Variety, February 18, 2018, 38.

2   Gérard Lefort, "Wim Wenders, son désir d'ailes," *Libération*, May 18, 1987, quoted in
    Der Himmel über Berlin: Ein Film von Wim Wenders. Presseheft. Munich: Filmverlag der
    Autoren, 1987), 25 (Deutsche Kinemathek Berlin, Schriftgutsammlung, folder 11404).
    Pauline Kael, "The Current Cinema. Zone Poem," *The New Yorker*, May 30, 1988, 77–79;
    here 78.

3   bell hooks, "Representing Whiteness. *Seeing Wings of Desire*," in *Yearning: Race, Gender,
    and Cultural Politics* (Boston: South End Press, 1990), 165–71.

4   "'Den Himmel wenigstens können sie nicht zerteilen,' sagte Manfred spöttisch. [...]
    'Doch,' sagte sie leise. 'Der Himmel teilt sich zuerst.'" Christa Wolf, *Der geteilte Himmel*
    (1963; Stuttgart: Deutscher Taschenbuchverlag, 1973), 223.

5   Deutsche Kinemathek Berlin, Schriftgutsammlung, folder 4.4-84107, 61.

6   "Der Himmel über Berlin. Ein Film von Wim Wenders." Draft script dated October
    1, 1986. Österreichisches Literaturarchiv Wien, Sammlung Peter Handke / Leihgabe
    Widrich, folder LW/W167.

7   Wim Wenders, Peter Handke, *Der Himmel über Berlin: Ein Filmbuch* (Frankfurt/Main:
    Suhrkamp, 1987), 46.

8   Wenders/Handke, *Filmbuch*, 91.

9   Wenders, "The American Dream" (1984), in Wim Wenders, *Emotion Pictures: Reflections
    on the Cinema*, trans. Sean Whiteside and Michael Hofmann (London: Faber and Faber,
    1989), 117–46; here 122. Caps in the original.

10 Wenders, "The American Dream," 143.

11 Wenders, "The American Dream," 138.

12 Wenders, "The American Dream," 146.

13 Wim Wenders, "Talking about Germany," [Kammerspiele Munich, November 10, 1991],
    in *The Cinema of Wim Wenders: Image, Narrative, and the Postmodern Condition*, ed. Roger
    F. Cook and Gerd Gemünden (Detroit: Wayne State UP, 1997), 51–59; here 54.

14 Wenders, "Talking about Germany," 59.

15 Wenders, "Talking about Germany," 55.

16 Wim Wenders, "An Attempted Description of an Indescribable Film," in *The Logic of
    Images*, trans. Michael Hofmann (London: Faber & Faber, 1991), 73–83; here 74.

17 Wenders, "Talking about Germany," 55.

18 Wenders, "An Attempted Description," 74. Caps in the original.

19 Wenders/Handke, *Filmbuch*, 122.

20 Wenders, "An Attempted Description," 74.

21 In the printed script, the sentence is in German: "Wie soll ich leben?" Wenders/Handke, *Filmbuch*, 47.

22 Michael Corvino, "Wim Wenders: A World-Wide Homesickness," *Film Quarterly* 31. 2 (Winter 1977–78): 9–19; here 10.

23 Charles H. Helmetag, "'. . . Of Men and Angels': Literary Allusions in Wim Wenders's *Wings of Desire*," *Literature/Film Quarterly* 18.4 (1990): 251–53.

24 Wenders/Handke, *Filmbuch*, 13–14.

25 Deutsches Literaturarchiv Marbach, A: Peter Handke, Notizbuch 50 (Aug. 28–Nov. 24, 1986): 66–69.

26 Linda C. Ehrlich, "Meditations on Wim Wenders's *Wings of Desire*," *Literature/Film Quarterly* 19. 4 (1991): 242–46; here 244.

27 Wenders/Handke, *Filmbuch*, 11.

28 Translated by A. S. Kline, https://www.poetryintranslation.com/PITBR/German/Rilke.php (accessed November 28, 2018). German original in Deutsche Kinemathek Berlin, Schriftgutsammlung, folder 4.4-84107, 61.

29 Wenders, "An Attempted Description," 74.

30 Coco Fusco, "Angels, History and Poetic Fantasy: An Interview with Wim Wenders," *Cinéaste* 16.4 (1987): 14–17; here 16.

31 Deutsches Literaturarchiv Marbach, A: Peter Handke, Notebook 50 (Aug. 28–Nov. 24, 1986): 28–79.

32 Deutsches Literaturarchiv Marbach, A: Suhrkamp Verlag, Siegfried Unseld Archiv: Peter Handke, "Zu den Homer-Szenen: 'Engel der Erzählung.'"

33 Wenders, "An Attempted Description," 77.

34 Wenders/Handke, *Filmbuch*, 135.

35 Wenders/Handke, *Filmbuch*, 67–68.

36 Wim Wenders, "Talking about Germany," 55.

37 I am grateful to Steven Wychorski for his help in identifying these musical moments.

38 Wenders/Handke, *Filmbuch*, 66.

39 Wenders/Handke, *Filmbuch*, 94.

40 Wenders/Handke, *Filmbuch*, 42.

41 Wenders/Handke, *Filmbuch*, 49.

42 Wenders/Handke, *Filmbuch*, 116.

43 Christian Rogowski, "'Der liebevolle Blick'? The Problem of Perception in Wim Wenders's *Wings* of *Desire*," *Seminar* 29.4 (November 1993): 398–409; here 407.

44 Deutsches Literaturarchiv Marbach, A: Suhrkamp Verlag, Siegfried Unseld Archiv: Peter Handke, "Zu den Homer-Szenen: 'Engel der Erzählung,'" 1–2.

45 Wolfram Schütte, "Niederfahrt zu den Menschen. *Der Himmel über Berlin*: der neue Film von Wim Wenders," *Frankfurter Rundschau*, October 29, 1987, 23.

46 "Erst das Staunen / über uns zwei, / das Staunen über den Mann und die Frau / hat mich zum Menschen gemacht." (Wenders/Handke, *Filmbuch*, 167).

47 The lyrics themselves are a punning allusion to the famous film by Fred Zinnemann, *From Here to Eternity* (1953).

48 "Walter Benjamin kaufte 1921 Paul Klees Aquarell *Angelus Novus* . . . In seiner letzten Schrift *Über den Begriff der Geschichte* (1940), interpretierte er das Bild als Allegorie des Rückblicks auf die Geschichte." (Wenders/Handke, *Filmbuch*, 23).

49 Xavier Vila and Alice Kuzniar, "Witnessing Narration in *Wings of Desire*," *Film Criticism*, 16.3 (Spring 1992): 53–65; here 62.

50 Wenders/Handke, *Filmbuch*, 28.

51 Wenders/Handke, *Filmbuch*, 58.

52 See, for instance, Katherine Dieckmann, "Wim Wenders: An Interview," *Film Quarterly* 38, no. 2 (Winter 1984–85): 2–7.

53 Wenders/Handke, *Filmbuch*, 140.

54 Wenders/Handke, *Filmbuch*, 146.

55 Wenders/Handke, *Filmbuch*, 151.

56 "Eines Tages, ich erinnere mich noch, hat hier der Gletscher gekalbt, und die Eisberge segelten nach Norden. Einmal trieb ein Baumstamm vorbei, noch grün, mit einem leeren Vogelnest. Myriaden von Jahren waren nur die Fische gesprungen!" (Wenders/Handke, *Filmbuch*, 83).

57 "Aber auch die erste [Geschichte], die vom Gras, von der Luft, von der Sonne, von den Luftsprüngen und den Ausrufen, dauert noch an." (Wenders/Handke, *Filmbuch*, 84).

58 Wenders/Handke, *Filmbuch*, 168.

59 "Nennt mir die Männer und Frauen und Kinder, die mich suchen werden, mich, ihren Erzähler wie sonst nichts auf der Welt." (Wenders/Handke, *Filmbuch*, 169).

60 Deutsches Literaturarchiv Marbach, A: Suhrkamp Verlag, Siegfried Unseld Archiv: Peter Handke, "Zu den Homer-Szenen: 'Engel der Erzählung,'" 32.

61 See Florent Gaudez, "Nous sommes embarqués. Le pari de l'embarquement socio-anthropologique. Pistes théoriques, pratiques, heuristiques," *Socio-anthropologie* 27 (2013): 147–53.

62 The later film also closes with the same words, again uttered by Curt Bois.

ACKNOWLEDGMENTS

The research for this book was supported by a grant from the Amherst College Faculty Research Award Program, funded by the H. Axel Schupf '57 Fund for Intellectual Life. The program allowed me to spend several months in Berlin, where the bulk of the present study was written, in the Staatsbibliothek near Potsdamer Platz, where Wenders's angels reside. Joan Murphy, Ulrich Nowka, and Julie and Francis Nowka Murphy graciously welcomed me into their home. I am grateful to my "Berlin family" for their hospitality, generosity, kindness, and interest in my work, and I cherish our many conversations into the wee hours of the night. Joan and Uli shared with me their vast knowledge of Berlin, and Joan deserves a special shout-out for providing me with useful feedback on my draft manuscript.

Thanks are due to the staff at the Deutsche Kinemathek Museum für Film und Fernsehen Berlin, including the Schriftgutarchiv (Regina Hoffmann, Lisa Roth), the Nachlassarchiv (Gerrit Thies), the Fotoarchiv (Julia Riedel), and the Periodicals Collection (Cordula Döhrer), who offered valuable, non-bureaucratic, and courteous support. Likewise, the staffs at the Deutsches Literaturarchiv Marbach am Neckar (Heidrun Fink, Thomas Kemme) and the Literaturarchiv at the Österreichische Nationalbibliothek Wien (Andreas Handler) made my brief respective research visits extremely productive. In Berlin, Gerd Gemünden helped arrange for me to attend the screening of the digitally restored version of *Wings of Desire* at the 2018 Berlin Film Festival. Philipp Stiasny of CineGraph Babelsberg generously shared his encyclopedic knowledge of, and enthusiasm for, German film history and Berlin trivia. Heike Klapdor offered useful feedback on my project in extended conversations and in her insightful comments on a draft version of the text. In the "Happy Valley" of the Five College Consortium, I have benefitted from collegial exchanges with, among others, Amelie Hastie (Amherst College), Barton Byg and Ela Gezen (University of Massachusetts, Amherst), and Joel Westerdale (Smith College). Jim Walker, editor at Camden House, has shepherded this project along with consummate patience and kindness. Most importantly, as always, I am deeply grateful to my wife, Nona Monahin, for her unwavering love and support over many years and for her more-than-angelic patience when it comes to proof reading. Whatever flaws this brief book may have, however, are entirely my own responsibility.